Spirit Filled Catholic Bible Study Series

Have Faith in God Bible Study

BIBLE STUDY

By: Marybeth Wuenschel

Edited by Susie Hughes

Spirit Filled Catholic

The Victory that Conquers the world is our Faith - 1 John 5:4

Have Faith in God

Spirit Filled Catholic Bible Study Series

This Bible Study comes with complementary access to **Online Video Course**
To access this course, click on link below
https://www.spiritfilledcatholic.com/havefaith

There is a wrap up teaching video for each week.
Don't miss it.

Follow me on Facebook https://www.facebook.com/catholicdevotional

Contact me - mbwuenschel@gmail.com

To subscribe to my blog and contact list go to
https://www.spiritfilledcatholic.com

Catechism of Catholic Church	CCC
Bible Readings - New American Bible Revised Edition	NAB
- New Living Translation	NLT

ACKNOWLEDGEMENTS
Sheila Lovelace - Editing and Review
Sherrie Nicolet - Final Editing and Review

Have Faith in God

Spirit Filled Catholic

Table of Contents

HOW TO APPROACH THIS BIBLE STUDY

Over the next 15 weeks, we will study Faith. Together we will explore the scriptures with the Holy Spirit. Jesus says....

> *"One does not live by bread alone,*
> *but by every word that comes forth from the mouth of God."* **Matthew 4:4**

We need to feed our soul as often as we feed our physical body. Our souls are hungry. As a matter of fact, they are dying of hunger. We cannot live without the word of God. God provided the Israelites manna every day in the desert. Jesus is our manna.
Jesus said....

> *"I am the bread of life;*
> *whoever comes to me will never hunger*
> *and he who believes in me will never thirst."* **John 6:35**

Vatican II Document, Dei Verbum quotes one of the greatest Bible Scholars of the Early Church, St. Jerome, to emphasize the need for all Christians to become intimately familiar with Scripture: "For ignorance of Scriptures is ignorance of Christ."

You are interested in this Bible study because you are seeking God.
The Bible says:

> "Seek first the Kingdom of God and His righteousness, and all these things will be given you besides." **Matthew 6:33** "Seek the Lord while he may be found." **Isaiah 55:6** "He who seeks me finds me when he seeks me with all his heart." **Jeremiah 29:13**

God says again in **Hebrews 11:6**, that He rewards those who seek him. Trust that as you spend time reading, studying, and discussing God's Word, you are choosing to spend time with God. He will grow you up in wisdom and faith. As you seek Him in His Word, He will make himself known to you. God promises to show you wonders beyond your wildest imagination (see **Jeremiah 33:3**).

The Bible says faith comes by hearing the Word of God (see **Romans 10:17**). Are you ready to see your faith increase? Your faith will grow as you read God's word daily. So, let us be committed to read the Bible every day and determined to nourish our spirits. Let's get hungry for God and His Word.

Father, we ask you to fill us with a hunger for You and Your Word. May we long for you as much as you long for us. We pray in faith and in the name of Jesus, AMEN.

We need the Holy Spirit for this Bible Study to be meaningful and effective!

The Holy Spirit is the most important part of Bible Study.

<u>Jesus says In John 14:26,</u> *"The Advocate, the Holy Spirit that the Father will send in my name – He will teach you EVERYTHING and remind you of all that I told you"(emphasis mine)."*

<u>Jesus says again in John 16:13,</u> *"But when he comes, the Spirit of truth, he will guide you into all truth."*

- Pray. The Holy Spirit will open up the Word for you and bring it to life, giving you wisdom, knowledge and understanding. Pray the following prayer, or one like it, every time you open the Bible or sit down to read or study.

    "Holy Spirit, I come to you and ask you to give me a hunger for your word and make it come alive. Lead me, guide me and give me understanding. Fill me, Holy Spirit to overflowing so that rivers of living water may flow out from me to a dry and thirsty world beginning with my very own life and family."

- This Bible Study is designed for weekly discussion groups or gatherings but may be done individually as well, or used as a daily devotional. If you are part of a discussion group, try to do your study daily so you and your discussion group will get more out of it.

- The questions are simply a guide. Let them be just a beginning. This Bible Study is for your spiritual growth and our growth as a community. Highlight those questions you found meaningful, so you will remember to share, especially if your discussion time is cut short.

- Feel free to follow the Holy Spirit as you read and answer the questions. If you follow the Holy Spirit instead of worrying about getting the correct answer, He will take you on a journey and you will have something to share. Use the margins to write down what you are learning and what the Holy Spirit is revealing to you as you pray, read, and share.

    <u>Bible study is…</u>
    * Reading the Word of God
    * Understanding the Word of God
    * Discussing the Word of God
    * Obeying or "Doing" the Word of God

    Be doers of the word and not hearers only, deluding yourselves. But the one who peers into the perfect law of freedom and perseveres, and is not a hearer who forgets but a doer who acts, such a one shall be blessed in what he does. **James 1:22, 25**

FAITH WEEK 1   Description of Faith

Come Holy Spirit, open up my heart to hear your Word and understand it.
Help me to be a doer, not just a hearer of Your Word. I invite You Holy Spirit to teach me.
May Your Word come alive and minister to me Your mercy, peace,
forgiveness, healing, joy, hope, love, and faith in You.

DAY 1

READ Hebrews 11:1-6, and 2 Corinthians 4:18

1.   Based on what these scriptures say, write your definition of Faith.

2.   According to Hebrews 11:3 how was the universe created (ordered)? (See also Genesis 1:1-3 and John 1:3)

3.   How do you fix your eyes on, or look at, something that can't be seen? Share how this is possible.

4.   Where does faith come from? How do we get it? (See scripture verses below)

READ   1 Corinthians 12: 7-9   _____

READ   Romans 12:3   _____

READ   Romans 10:17   _____

Faith is supernatural. It believes in something you can't see, feel, taste, hear, or smell. Faith makes no sense in this physical realm. It may make no sense to those around you, and may be impossible to explain. Faith is believing without proof. Faith is knowing you have it, even though you can't see it. Faith is the proof, or the substance of things hoped for, as Hebrews 11:1 says. Faith is the title-deed to the property you know you own even though you don't yet have it in your possession.

Faith is expecting God to do what He says He will do PERIOD. Faith is believing God's word to be true and acting on it. Faith is believing in God's promises, His love for you and His faithfulness. Faith is believing in God's love for you no, matter what it looks like and no matter what you have done. Faith comes as a gift from God. God has deposited in us, through the Holy Spirit, a measure of faith.

We need to use it and exercise it and watch it become a habit. Practice trusting God. Our default nature is to trust what we see, hear, smell and feel. Practice letting go and trusting God, while tuning your ears to receive His promptings and nudges.

Faith is both a gift of the Holy Spirit and a fruit of the Holy Spirit. As we walk with the Holy Spirit, faith comes. We can't remain in the physical realm and enjoy the fruit of the supernatural realm. We have to venture into the promised land, into the unknown and unseen realm of God. Faith comes, the Bible says, from hearing God's word. You have chosen to study God's word, so watch your faith in Him grow as you persevere in it. Don't follow others; follow the Holy Spirit. Stay in the Bible. Seek Him in His word and you will never go wrong.

DAY 2

READ   Matthew 7: 24-29 The Two Foundations

   1.   Describe the difference between the foolish and wise man.

READ   Matthew 6:25-34 and Philippians 4:4-7   Dependence on God

   2.   Write this story down in a journal or paste it on your mirror. Choose a verse you may want to memorize! What is this passage teaching us?

DAY 3
READ Matthew 15:21-28   The Canaanite Woman

1.   What do we learn about Jesus?

2.   What do we learn about the Canaanite woman?

3.   Why does Jesus respond as He does in verse 24 and 26? (Read Matthew 10:5-10 and Matthew 28:19)

4.   Why do you think she is referred to as the Canaanite woman?

5.   In Verse 28 Jesus describes her faith as "GREAT." What made her faith great?

6.   Do this woman's actions shock you? Would you do what she did? Do we approach Jesus like this? May we?

DAY 4

READ   Luke 18:1-8   The Parable of the Persistent Widow

1.   What is the purpose of this passage? (See verse 1)

2.   Do we approach God like this? May we?

3.   What was the outcome for the woman, for us?

READ   Luke 11: 5-13 Teachings on Prayer

4.   What does God promise us and why?

DAY 5

READ   Mark 4:35-41   Disciples in the Storm

1.   How do the disciples voice their lack of faith? Write their words here.

2.   How might their words offend Jesus? (See 1 Peter 5:7

3.   What does Jesus do/say to the wind and the waves?

4.   What were they afraid of at first and then finally?

5.   What is Jesus asking of His disciples? Does Jesus expect a lot from them; from us?

6.   What are some winds and waves that can really rock a person's world?

OPTIONAL READ another account of this story Luke 8:22-25

If you don't have peace it's not God's fault. He gives peace. He brings peace. He is peace. If you don't have peace, you simply aren't following Him. You aren't rooted in Him. The good news is you still can be!

"Have no anxiety at all, but in everything, by prayer and petition, with thanksgiving, make your requests known to God. Then the peace of God that surpasses all understanding will guard your hearts and minds in Christ Jesus." **Philippians 4:6-7**

If you are worried or anxious, you are trusting and leaning on yourself or your past and you doubt God will come through for you. You doubt God's love for you. You doubt. Everyone in the boat with Jesus feared for their lives when the boat took on water during the storm. They doubted God. They forgot God was in their boat. Have you forgotten?

Is Jesus in your boat? Does Jesus live in your home, in your marriage, in your workplace? Is Jesus Lord of your home, your marriage, your finances, your health? Have you invited Him? If so, then rest assured that you are in good hands. Jesus is in YOUR boat. What have you to fear? Your resources will not run dry, because your source never runs dry. You will not be left without.

"The Lord is my shepherd, I shall not want, He makes me lie down in green pastures.....He leads me beside quiet waters." **Psalm 23**.

He does not lead us beside turbulent waters; for some reason we go there enough on our own. We don't need God for that. He does, however, lead us to safe harbors, green pastures, quiet waters. Of this we can be sure, and Jesus made it clear when the disciples asked, "don't you care?" He was short with them for believing such a thing. So, today be determined to believe our God is good, and wants good things for us. Believe that He does care.

DAY 6

    1.   Fill in ......

<table>
<tr><td></td><td>**Who believed?**</td><td>**What did they believe?**</td></tr>
<tr><td>Genesis 15:4-6</td><td>_____</td><td>_____</td></tr>
<tr><td></td><td></td><td>_____</td></tr>
<tr><td>Jonah 3:3-5</td><td>_____</td><td>_____</td></tr>
<tr><td></td><td></td><td>_____</td></tr>
<tr><td>Hebrews 11:7</td><td>_____</td><td>_____</td></tr>
<tr><td></td><td></td><td>_____</td></tr>
</table>

READ Reflection on the following pages

    2.   Comment:

Reflection

The Challenge for us as Christians is To Follow Jesus…..

* When we can see Him and when we can't.
* When we hear Him and when we don't.
* When we know what's coming just ahead and when we don't.
* When we feel His presence and when we don't.
* When we are certain He has our back and when we aren't.
* When we feel like it and when we don't.

The challenge for us as Christians is to follow Jesus to the mountain tops and even to the depths, when we feel like it and when we don't. Faith is trusting Jesus to come through for us even when everything we are experiencing or witnessing says the opposite. Faith is more than believing IN Jesus but believing HIM. Like Abraham, we are called to believe Him, to believe His words, to believe that what He says will really happen. The Bible says that Abraham believed God, and it was credited to him as righteousness. He believed that what God said was true and good and he believed it would actually happen.

Faith is being persistent, not giving up even when the report from the doctor is bleak. Faith is believing not only that God CAN, but that God WILL. Most people believe that God can do anything, that nothing is too difficult for God. It doesn't require faith to believe God CAN. Faith is required to believe God WILL. Our challenge is to believe that God loves us and WILL come through for us; no matter what we are going through and no matter what the world says or believes.

The Canaanite Woman

Jesus describes the woman in this story as a woman of "GREAT FAITH." Wow, if only Jesus would think that way of me! How does she earn such praise from the One and Only? What does she do to earn the respect of our Lord? (By the way, Jesus uses the term "great" to describe someone's faith only one other time.) She pursues Jesus for the sake of her daughter and doesn't take "no" for an answer! We give up too easily. We do! All of us, not just you, me, but most of us. We hear one bad report, and we sigh and fear creeps in, and we give in to the "inevitable." Not this woman. She knew where to go and wasn't afraid to go there. My goal is to never back down no matter what the report. My goal is not to give up trusting in God.

Not only was the Canaanite woman persistent, but also confident. She didn't let who she was, or what other's thought she deserved, prevent her from going for it. She knew it was not her place to ask, but she asked anyway. She didn't let her "low" position keep her from receiving the best from God.

I make it a rule never to sigh and say "Oh well, it must be God's will" when praying for my health or someone else's. My job is to ask, to keep on asking, to trust and to keep on trusting. When we pray for God's will to be done, in the case of someone's health, prayer usually stops in its tracks. It's hard to keep on asking when someone just prayed "but God, your will be done," because if we continue, we might be praying against God's will.

We all have a tendency to do this. When we say "but your will be done," regarding healing, it is usually because we don't want to be disappointed, we don't want the person we are praying for to be disappointed, or we don't want to look bad or feel foolish by praying for something that might not happen. Usually, we just don't know what else to pray. It just seems right. When you don't know how to pray, ask the Holy Spirit how to pray. He will never lead you astray. "For we do not know how to pray as we ought, but the Spirit itself intercedes with inexpressible groanings." Romans 8:26.

Of course, God's will is important, and God wants us to pray according to His will because His will is perfect and always right. We should pray for God's will when looking for a new car, or when debating whether or not to move, take a new job, or where to send your kids to college. He knows what is best for us and wants what is best. However, when it comes to healing, I choose to believe healing IS His will. It is always God's will to heal. He never said no. When Jesus walked on the earth, He healed them all. He healed all who came to him. He never once said no, and He has not changed His mind.

One evening after Bible Study, a man came in, I recognized him, he worked for the church taking care of the facilities part time. He came asking for prayer.

He said, "I have just been diagnosed with stage 4 cancer." I saw the fear and pain in his face. We began to pray for him; there were 2 or 3 of us. I remember feeling the Holy Spirit, and I just blurted out. "Mike, (I think that was his name) did you know that in the gospels, no one ever came up to Jesus asking, 'Lord just give me the strength to get through this.' No one! They always asked for the healing." He didn't quite hear what I said. He told me "Oh no that's all I want, I just want God to give me strength." As soon as he said that, we laid our hands on Him to pray and I said, "Well I pray that stage 4 cancer goes to stage 0 in the name of Jesus."

His next doctor's visit showed the cancer had been reduced to stage 1 without any treatment. I saw him Easter Sunday at Mass as jubilant as a child, and we hugged. He knew it was prayer. He knew it was God!

Even if it is God's will for us to be sick and die, our job is to pray, to ask, to intercede on each other's behalf, to believe when our sick friends are too tired and ill to believe for themselves.

David prayed for his son to be healed, for God to spare his son's life (see 2 Samuel 12). God passed judgment on David by David's own lips. God decided to take his son. David prayed fervently. He did not eat but spent the nights prostrate before God. It was God's will to take his son, but that did not keep David from seeking the Lord on his son's behalf.

Does a lifeguard give up swimming to the rescue, or is the drowning swimmer worth his or her effort? It may be God's will to take that swimmer, but it is not the lifeguard's decision. That is how I want to approach prayer.

I am challenging us to pray as if a life depends on it, both spiritually and/or physically. That is what I want to do. I want to grow in my prayer life. I want to be fervent in my prayer to God. I don't mean spending hours fervently on my knees, but following the Holy Spirit and praying until peace comes. Sometimes that may mean just remembering someone to the Lord as Paul does in Romans 1:9-10. I have a long way to go, but the Canaanite woman in this passage encourages me.

My challenge to you today is to go out on a limb and be willing to look foolish. It may be worth it. You never know unless you try.

NOTES

FAITH WEEK 2   Your Faith has Healed You

A prayer for you ... I keep asking that the God of our Lord Jesus Christ, the glorious Father, may give you the Spirit of wisdom and revelation, so that you may know him better. I pray that the eyes of your heart may be enlightened in order that you may know the hope to which he has called you, the riches of his glorious inheritance in his holy people, and his incomparably great power for us who believe.....
Ephesians 1:17-19

❖—◆—❖

DAY 1

Put the scripture passage above to prayer for yourself and/or a loved one. Pray first by placing your name in prayer, then pray it again with your loved one's name. Replace "you" with the name of your husband, child, mother, sister, etc. **See prayer sample below.**

I ask you God of our Lord Jesus Christ, glorious Father to give **(me or add the name of a loved one)** *the Spirit of wisdom and revelation so that I may know you better. I also pray Father in the name of Jesus that my heart be enlightened in order that I may have hope in you and that I may know the riches of my inheritance from you and the power for me as a believer*

DAY 2

READ   Mark 5:21-34   Woman with a Hemorrhage

1.   In whom or what was the woman's faith in all those years?

2.   What may have lead her to approach Jesus?

3.   What happened when she turned to Jesus and touched His cloak? What did she believe would happen?

4.   What does it mean "Power went out of him?" Where or what was the power coming from Him? (see Luke 5:17, Luke 6:19, 1 Sam 16:13, Judges 14:19, and 1 Kings 18:46)

5.   Why did Jesus concern himself with this woman even while a little girl was dying and waiting for him? What does this teach you about Jesus?

The passage of the woman with the hemorrhage is so moving because we learn so much about Jesus. Jesus does not play favorites. He does not discriminate between the rich and poor, gentile or Jew, slave or free, male or female, neither does He show favoritism between the OLD and YOUNG. So many times, we discount the elderly, but Jesus doesn't. He loves us even in our old age. There was a young girl dying yet Jesus stopped the procession to heal an older woman. Everyone is important to Jesus. He knows that just because you are growing older or are less useful than others, it doesn't mean you don't deserve to be healed as much as a little girl. I love that about this passage!!!

This woman wasted all her money and time, (12 YEARS) trusting in doctors who could do nothing for her. Her faith was in the doctors. She believed in them, obviously, since she spent everything she had on them. When she shifted her faith from the doctors to Jesus, she sought out Jesus and came to him. When she came to Him, He didn't say "What took you so long?"

Jesus didn't even make her wait. He called her a woman of faith. He praised her faith and told her it was her faith that made her well. He didn't expect her to prove her faith; her present amount of faith was enough. She had faith in Him today, He didn't care that all her yesterdays may have been faithless. What a God we serve! He accepts us today, just the way we are.

DAY 3
READ Luke 18:35-43 The Blind Man

1.   How does the blind man show his faith? What is extraordinary about him?

2.   What does Jesus ask the blind man and why?

3.   Why is Jesus referred to as the Son of David? (See Jeremiah 23:5-6 and Matthew 1:1-17)

THE BLIND MAN hears the commotion and asks the passers-by what is happening. They tell him Jesus is coming. He calls out to Jesus, and Jesus stops everything. This man is bold! Can you imagine interrupting a bishop or the pope? Jesus is GOD. Yet the blind man has the audacity to do just that. Jesus asks him "What is it you want?" and the blind man answers, "I want to see."

 Is that the right thing to ask? May we really ask Jesus for something so personal as "I want to see" or "I want to be healed" or should we pray for more noble causes, such as peace in Israel, the cure for cancer, etc. Maybe the beggar should have been more concerned with others than himself. Maybe he should have asked Jesus for something more important like freedom from Roman occupation or a cure for leprosy!

Instead, when the blind man gets an audience with the KING OF KINGS, he says "I want to see." He has Jesus' full attention, and he takes advantage of it, and Jesus recognizes it as FAITH, and He heals him! The blind Man's name, (we learn later in Mark, another account of the same story), is Bartimaeus. Bartimaeus means "Son of Timaeus" He wasn't even worthy of a first name, he was only known as "son of...."But today because of his boldness and because JESUS made a place for him in history, he is known for all eternity as "BARTIMAEUS."

DAY 4
READ   Mark 5: 21-24, and 35-43 Jairus' Daughter
1.   What did Jesus say to the father? See verse 36.

2.   What is Jesus teaching us about faith in Him? What are His expectations regarding that faith?

Jesus said to Jairus, "Just have faith." He expected Jairus to have faith after hearing the news that his daughter had just died. Jesus didn't let him digest this news. He didn't give him time to feel or even think. Faith? Faith in what? My daughter is dead and you want me to have faith? If the answer to prayer is slow in coming, it doesn't mean you are given leave to trust in something or someone else. Don't veer off. Stay tuned-in to Jesus. He is not done with you yet. Jairus could have chosen to listen to the messengers who said, "Don't trouble the teacher any longer," but he didn't quit listening to Jesus. Don't let the bad report cause you to veer off the road.

Don't quit praying; don't quit asking; don't quit believing; don't quit expecting.

Imagine the surprise, the overwhelming joy, in the house of Jairus. Their daughter was dying, then she died, and is now miraculously alive again. What an astonishing thing to witness, right in their very own home. Imagine what it feels like to be so highly favored by God, that He would visit your home at the time of your greatest need. Imagine feeling so special. Imagine the relief and the joy that their daughter was restored to them by the goodness of GOD, the creator of the world, the awesome God who by His word created the heavens and the earth and the awesome wonder that this same God thinks of them and moves on their behalf. Oh, the unspeakable joy!

God wants to do the same for you. He wants to shower His favor, love, and joy on you. He wants to overwhelm you, to show up in your home and work wonders for you and your family because He loves you because you are His. No matter what has happened, no matter how bad it is, or how long it is taking, call to Him and keep calling: don't give up. He has so much more for you. Remember, God doesn't have favorites. He doesn't love one of us more than another. He wants it for you just like He wanted it for this young girl. You are just as special to God.

Another point worth mentioning, Jesus gave strict orders that no one should know (Mark 5:43). He was not doing this for His Glory or even for His Father's Glory. Maybe He did it for them because He loves them.

John 5:19-20 Jesus answered and said to them,
"Amen, amen, I say to you, a son cannot do anything on his own, but only what he sees his father doing; for what he does, his son will do also. For the Father loves his son and shows him everything that he himself does, and he will show him greater works than these, so that you may be amazed."

DAY 5

READ   John 5:19-30

1.   Highlight the word "LIFE"each time it occurs.

RE-READ   John 5:19-26

2.   What does this passage say about life and death?

3.   How do we honor the Father?

4.   Describe the relationship between the Father and the Son? (See John 14:9-14, Colossians 2:9-10, 1 Corinthians 1:24)

5.   What does it mean "Whoever does not honor the Son does not honor the Father who sent him" (See also John 8:42, 1 John 2:23, 5:1)

DAY 6

READ   Acts 20:7-12 and READ 1 Kings 17:17-24

1.   Describe what happens in each. How are they similar?

READ   Luke 7:11-17, and Acts 9:36-43

2.   Describe what happens in each. How are they similar?

3.   Comment on any or all of the above accounts.

NOTES

FAITH WEEK 3   Faith of the Community

"For this reason I kneel before the Father, from whom every family in heaven and on earth derives its name. I pray that out of his glorious riches he may strengthen you with power through his Spirit in your inner being, so that Christ may dwell in your hearts through faith. And I pray that you, being rooted and established in love, may have power, together with all the Lord's holy people, to grasp how wide and long and high and deep is the love of Christ, and to know this love that surpasses knowledge–that you may be filled to the measure of all the fullness of God."   EPH. 3:14-19

❧ ❧ ❧

I kneel before you Father and pray that you will strengthen me with your power through the Holy Spirit in my inner being. I pray that Christ will dwell in my heart and that I will become rooted and grounded in love. I want to look like you Lord, and act like you.

DAY 1

READ   Mark 2:1-12   "Four friends through the Roof"

1.   Whose faith did Jesus see? Describe their faith.

2.   What does this say about community?

3.   How far will you go, or what will you do, to get someone to Jesus.

4.   Did his sins make him a paralytic? See John 9:1-7

DAY 2

READ   Acts 2:42-47, and 4:23-37

    1.   List the qualities/responsibilities/practices of a faith-filled community (See also Acts 1:14, and Matthew 28:19-20)

    2.   Summarize what religion was like in the early Church.

DAY 3

READ   Luke 4: 14-30, see also (Mark 6:1-6)

    1.   How was Jesus fulfilling the Isaiah Scripture? (See Luke 7:21-22)

    2.   What two prophets does Jesus mention? (see verses 24-27)

    3.   Why does Jesus bring up these two accounts?   What is He suggesting?

    4.   Why were the people so furious?

DAY 4

READ   1 Kings 17:7-16   "Elijah and the Widow"

1.   Describe what happened.

2.   How does the widow show her faith?

3.   COMMENT.

Recently I was on a plane and there was a delay for some reason; mechanical, weather, crew issue, air traffic congestion, whatever. It doesn't matter. All I knew was, the plane didn't take off on time and we were waiting. I didn't know the reason and didn't have the whole picture. The traffic controller in the tower has that information. He knows traffic patterns, mechanical difficulties, and is aware of traffic congestion.

Many times, they do have to delay a flight in order to avoid collisions. And it occurred to me that it's similar with God. We ask for things and sometimes have to wait. We don't always know the reason; we don't have the whole picture. If we are living in faith according to His will, He will guide us. Life does get confusing, unmanageable, frustrating, and uncertain at times. Things we don't understand, we might see as missed opportunities, unfortunate situations, or even bad luck. But if we're following His will and walking in His light, these could actually be part of His perfect plan for us.

Thomas Merton says in his book, The Seven Story Mountain, "It was in the hands of God. There was nothing I could do but leave myself to His mercy. But surely, by this time, I should have been able to realize that He is much more eager to take care of us, and capable of doing so, than we could be ourselves. It is only when we refuse His help, resist His will, that we have conflict, trouble, disorder, unhappiness, ruin. "We need to have faith and trust that He's in charge and knows what's best for us and that He is guiding us to a better life.

Written by: Kate Johnston

DAY 5
READ 2 Kings 5:1-14 "Cure of Naaman"

1. In whom did the slave girl have faith?

2. Why was the King of Israel nervous?

3. Why was Naaman angry?

4. What wisdom came from Naaman's servants?

5. How does this story give you hope?

READ Acts 5:12-16

6. Comment on the faith of the Community.

DAY 6
READ   Reflection.
1.   Comment about something you learned or found enlightening

Reflection:

The Paralytic "Four friends through the roof"

Jesus says, "Child your sins are forgiven." Jesus forgave him his sins. The four friends brought the paralytic to Jesus because he needed physical healing. However, Jesus knew the man's sins weighed heavily upon him. Jesus knew his greater need and desire was to be set free from the burden and slavery of sin. Have you recognized the slavery of sin? Have you ever noticed the bondage sin puts you in? Have you noticed how sin gets a hold of you and commands you to obey? We were made to love God and be with God. We were made to be one with God. Sin separates us from God. When we are separated from God, it causes us grief and pain because our souls were made to be one with God. We may not realize it, but we are in search of freedom from sin until we find Jesus, the one who frees us.

This paralytic may not have realized his greater need, but Jesus did. Jesus came to break the power and hold sin has on us. He did it when He died on the cross. He did it to set us free. Jesus had so much more in store for the paralytic, so much more than the physical healing he was searching for.

Are you sick, or is someone you love, sick? Take them to Jesus. Bear them on your shoulders. Be willing to go through a roof. Disturb your Pastor or Priest for prayer or the anointing of the sick with oil. Be bold! Be willing to interfere in someone's life who needs healing or forgiveness or maybe both. It may be cumbersome and uncomfortable to offer to take someone to Jesus or to stop what you are doing and pray with them or ask for them. It can be inconvenient to take someone to church, to invite someone to a prayer group, to the Sacrament of Reconciliation, or to a priest for the Sacrament of Anointing of the Sick. It may require a phone call or a knock on the door. It may require a visit to the hospital.

These four friends did not have a doubt in their hearts that Jesus was the answer for their friend. They walked toward Jesus confidently. It was worth it to them to pay whatever price would be required of them to see their friend healed. They loved their friend, and they knew Jesus would heal him. They did not settle for the disease. They wanted more for their friend, and they were not afraid to ask for it. *"Ask and you shall receive; seek and you will find; knock and the door will be opened to you"* **Luke 11:9**. Don't be limited by what others might think or the doctor's diagnosis. Bring it to God in prayer.

Are you sick? Well praise God, there is hope for you! God loves to be glorified through us when we are healed or when we pray for someone else (See John 14:13).

Are you a sinner in need of forgiveness? Jesus is always willing to forgive. YES ALWAYS! Are you sick and in need of healing? Jesus is always willing to heal.

1 John 1:9 *If we acknowledge our sins, he is faithful and just and will forgive our sins and cleanse us from every wrongdoing*

Matthew 8:3 *Jesus "stretched out his hand, touched him, and said I do will it. Be made clean." His leprosy was cleansed immediately.*

Did the paralytic's sins cause him to be sick? Many wonder about that. Did your sin cause you to be sick? This is always in the back of our minds, so I am going to address it. Did your sin cause this? Do you deserve it somehow? Did you eat poorly all your life? Did you smoke... Is this just your lot in life? Did you do something so bad that this is how you are paying for it? If this is somewhere in the back of your mind, like it is sometimes with me, then I have some really good news... Jesus already paid for that sin, so be free to go to Jesus for forgiveness and healing, just like the paralytic.

Jesus paid a mighty price to set us free from sin, so there is no use holding on to it. Be free! Your sin is not too great for Jesus. We think God will heal others but not us. We may think that his/her sin is more forgivable than mine. For some reason, our own sin is much worse in our eyes, but not in God's eyes. They are all the same to God. He took every sin, yours and mine. If we think our sin is too much for Jesus, then what more does Jesus have to do? What more is there? When we say our sin is too much for God, we are really saying that the cross was not enough.

He shouldn't have bothered to take the cross, since it just wasn't enough for my sins. Maybe if Jesus had suffered more, we would be satisfied. Jesus' death satisfied God completely, shouldn't it satisfy us? Well, the good news is your sins, horrid as they may be, were carried by Jesus to the cross.

NOTES

FAITH WEEK 4   Justification through Faith

"Come Holy Spirit, I invite you. I need You. Open up the Word for me, lead me, guide me and give me understanding. I come to You and ask You to give me a hunger for Your Word. Fill me Holy Spirit to overflowing that rivers of living water may flow out from me to a dry and thirsty world beginning with my very own life and family."

❧ ❧ ❧

DAY 1

READ   Ephesians 2:1-22 and Ephesians 1:3-14

1. Compare words or phrases in these passages that describe life with and without Christ.

WITH CHRIST	WITHOUT CHRIST

2. Comments?

DAY 2

READ   Catechism of the Catholic Church below

ccc**1990** Justification detaches man from sin which contradicts the love of God and purifies his heart of sin. Justification follows upon God's merciful initiative of offering forgiveness. It reconciles man with God. It frees from the enslavement to sin, and it heals.

ccc**1996** Our justification comes from the grace of God. Grace is favor, the free and undeserved help that God gives us to respond to his call to become children of God, adoptive sons, partakers of the divine nature and of eternal life.

JUSTIFY
Theology. To declare innocent or guiltless; absolve; acquit. *(dictionary.com)*

1.   What does justification mean in your own words?

READ   Galatians 2:15-21

2.   How are we justified, according to these verses and what does that mean for us?

RE-READ   Galatians 2:19-21

3.   What does it mean "for if justification comes through the law, then Christ died for nothing?"

Jesus lived the perfect life. His life fulfilled the law. Complete fulfillment of the law is the way to be justified before God. Complete fulfillment of the law is the way to be justified (set free, forgiven, made right, restored, made whole). No one except Jesus can fulfill the Law. We attempt to complete the requirements of the Law but fall short (Romans 3:23). If we could fulfill the law, than Jesus would not have needed to come to fulfill it and to die. Without the shedding of blood there is no forgiveness (Hebrews 9:22)

Jesus came not to abolish the Old Testament or the Law but to fulfill it. Jesus fulfilled the requirement of the law. God required perfection and the law to be obeyed perfectly. Only Jesus could obey the law perfectly and completely. He did it for us. Because of Jesus we get all the benefits of the Law and the Old Testament. We get all the Blessings and none of the Curses.

The Old Testament lays out the Law. If you obey all the commandments, you will be blessed. If you do not do everything the law requires, you will be cursed. Jesus fulfilled the law to such an extent that we now, through Him receive the blessings and not the curses. The Bible says that all of God's promises are yes and amen in Christ. Everything the Bible promises, Jesus accomplishes for us. He ends the law completely and it is now HIM. He is everything.

Written by: Mark Wuenschel

DAY 3

READ   Galatians 3:1-14

1. RE-READ Galatians 3:1-5. How do you receive the Spirit (Holy Spirit)?

2. What do you think Paul is admonishing them for?

3. Write down in the table below every word/phrase/adjective in this passage that has to do with spirit/faith and law/flesh (see Galatians 3:1-14 and Galatians 21-29)

SPIRIT/FAITH	LAW/FLESH

4. Read all the words/prases from the table above and explain in a brief statement the difference between the law and faith.

5.   Write out Galatians 3:6. What does it say/mean?

DAY 4

READ   Romans 3:19-20

New Living Translation	New American Bible
[19] Obviously, the law applies to those to whom it was given, for its purpose is to keep people from having excuses, and to show that the entire world is guilty before God. [20] For no one can ever be made right with God by doing what the law commands. The law simply shows us how sinful we are.	[19] Now we know that what the law[d] says is addressed to those under the law, so that every mouth may be silenced and the whole world stand accountable to God, [20] since no human being will be justified in his sight by observing the law; for through the law comes consciousness of sin.

1.   Based on the verses above, what is the purpose of the Law?

READ   Romans 3:21-31

New Living Translation	New American Bible
Christ Took Our Punishment 21 But now God has shown us a way to be made right with him without keeping the requirements of the law, as was promised in the writings of Moses and the prophets long ago. 22 We are made right with God by placing our faith in Jesus Christ. And this is true for everyone who believes, no matter who we are. 23 For everyone has sinned; we all fall short of God's glorious standard. 24 Yet God, in his grace, freely makes us right in his sight. He did this through Christ Jesus when he freed us from the penalty for our sins. 25 For God presented Jesus as the sacrifice for sin. People are made right with God when they believe that Jesus sacrificed his life, shedding his blood. This sacrifice shows that God was being fair when he held back and did not punish those who sinned in times past, 26 for he was looking ahead and including them in what he would do in this present time. God did this to demonstrate his righteousness, for he himself is fair and just, and he makes sinners right in his sight when they believe in Jesus. 27 Can we boast, then, that we have done anything to be accepted by God? No, because our acquittal is not based on obeying the law. It is based on faith. 28 So we are made right with God through faith and not by obeying the law. 29 After all, is God the God of the Jews only? Isn't he also the God of the Gentiles? Of course he is. 30 There is only one God, and he makes people right with himself only by faith, whether they are Jews or Gentiles. 31 Well then, if we emphasize faith, does this mean that we can forget about the law? Of course not! In fact, only when we have faith do we truly fulfill the law.	**III. Justification Through Faith in Christ** **Justification Apart from the Law.** 21 But now the righteousness of God has been manifested apart from the law, though testified to by the law and the prophets, 22 the righteousness of God through faith in Jesus Christ for all who believe. For there is no distinction; 23 all have sinned and are deprived of the glory of God. 24 They are justified freely by his grace through the redemption in Christ Jesus, 25 whom God set forth as an expiation, through faith, by his blood, to prove his righteousness because of the forgiveness of sins previously committed, 26 through the forbearance of God—to prove his righteousness in the present time, that he might be righteous and justify the one who has faith in Jesus. 27 What occasion is there then for boasting? It is ruled out. On what principle, that of works? No, rather on the principle of faith. 28 For we consider that a person is justified by faith apart from works of the law. 29 Does God belong to Jews alone? Does he not belong to Gentiles, too? Yes, also to Gentiles, 30 for God is one and will justify the circumcised on the basis of faith and the uncircumcised through faith. 31 Are we then annulling the law by this faith? Of course not! On the contrary, we are supporting the law.

2.   What does righteousness mean?

3.   Through whom do we get righteousness, and who receives it? (See also 2 Corinthians 5:21)

4.   Summarize this passage in your own words. (See notes in the New American Bible to Romans 3: 21-31)

FILL IN: Romans 3:21-25

But now the righteousness of God has been manifested apart from the _____,   though

testified to by the law and the prophets, the righteousness of God through _____ in

Jesus Christ for all who _____. For there is no distinction, all have _____

and are deprived of the glory of God. They are justified freely by His _____ through the

redemption in Christ Jesus, whom God set forth as an expiation, through _____ in His

_____.

5.   Please rewrite the passage above, (Romans 3:21-25) in your own words?

READ   Romans 5:1-2

Therefore, since we have been justified by _____, we have _____ with

God through our _____ _____ _____, through whom we

have gained access by _____ to this _____ in which we now

stand, and we boast in hope of the glory of God.

6.   Can you rewrite this passage above, (Romans 3:21-25) in your own words?

DAY 5

READ   Romans 4:1-5

1.   What is the difference between gift and wage?   Explain.

READ   Romans 4: 13-25

2.   Describe Abraham's faith in this passage. (See verses 17-22)

3.   How does verse 17 describe God?

4.   Romans 4:3 says that righteousness was credited to Abraham. What does that mean? (in your own words)

5.   What does Rom 4:22-25 say about us and righteousness?

6.   Comment on something you have learned in this passage

READ   Galatians 3:6-7

7.   Who are the children of Abraham?

The Bible tells us, Abraham was justified by faith, not by works. Abraham believed, and it was credited to him as righteousness. What made Abraham right with God? His faith in God made him right with God. If the Law made us righteous, or right with God, then Jesus didn't need to come and die. However, our righteousness does not depend on the Law. Obeying the Law does not justify us. The Law does not cleanse us.

Do you know that there is nothing in us that makes us righteous? God says our righteousness is like filthy rags to him. All of us have become like unclean men, and all our good deeds (or righteousness or righteous acts) are like polluted rags; we have all withered like leaves, and our guilt carries us away like the wind. Isaiah 64:5 (NAB) What does this mean? Is there anything we can do to earn heaven ourselves? The answer is: we do not have the means within ourselves to get to heaven. We need Jesus. He supplies all we need. This may seem odd to you. See John 15:5, where Jesus says without me; you can do nothing. He is our righteousness. This is the "GOOD NEWS" of Jesus Christ. He paid it all. He paved the way for us. We are righteous because we are clothed with Christ (from Galatians 3:27).

Romans goes on to say that if works made Abraham righteous, then he would have something to boast about, but not so in the sight of God. (Romans 4:2) For example, if we are justified on the basis of, how many times we go to church, how many daily masses we make, or how many prayers we pray, then we would be like the pharisee in the temple praying (see Luke 18). He prayed thanking God that he was not like that tax collector, I tithe, I... I... I... The pharisee listed all his good deeds before God, and the poor tax collector just bowed his head and said "Lord; I am a sinner." Jesus asked the disciples, "which one went home justified?" Which one went home right with God? The one who did everything correct and perfect according to the Law, or the one who confessed his sinfulness to God. Jesus said the tax collector was justified or was made right with the Lord, not the pharisee.

Fill in the words to the following passage below. (Romans 4: 13-17)

It was not through the _____ that the promise was made to Abraham and his

descendants that he would inherit the world, but through the _____

that comes from _____. For if those who adhere to the _____ are heirs,

_____ is null and the promise is void. For the _____ produces wrath; but

where there is no _____, neither is there violation.   For this reason, it depends

on _____, so that it may be a _____, and the promise may be

guaranteed to all his descendants, not to those who only adhere to the law but to those who

follow the_____ of Abraham, who is the _____ of us, as it is

written, "I have made you father of many _____." He is our father in the sight of

God, in whom he believed, who gives_____ to the dead and calls into being what does

not exist.

DAY 6
READ   Galatians 5:4-6
1.   Write out verse 4.

2.   Now re-write it in your own words.

3.   READ Reflections below and comment about something you learned or found enlightening.

Reflection

At the beginning of our journey with God, we are taught the Ten Commandments. We learn right from wrong, especially as children, and we believe that as long as we follow the Ten Commandments and are "good," we will go to Heaven. However, not one of us can completely follow the Ten Commandments. It doesn't matter how hard we try; we will fail. None of us can obey these commandments to the "T." At some point in our lives, we have, or we will, break at least one of the commandments!

So, what then?

We live in worry; we live in uncertainty; we live in fear because we don't know what fate has in store for us when we die. We wonder if we will receive His forgiveness. We hope that we have done enough good things to get us to Heaven. We are counting on the good things we have done to outweigh the bad and earn us access to eternal life.

Many of us, even though we become adults, stay with this type of mentality, living in fear and wonder, INDEFINITELY. We may even reach old age and die believing this is all there is. Our relationship with Jesus is still superficial. We have not invited Him into our lives or accepted Him as our Savior. What if there is more? What if there is so much, much more?

Jesus is calling us to grow; He is calling us to have a deeper relationship with Him. He is calling us to know Him better and learn all He has for us. We must make a decision to let Him in. I believe the sooner, the better. Christ Renews His Parish is a renewal process in the Catholic Church, and this is what the manual says regarding commitment to Jesus Christ.

CRHP
"Christianity did not begin with a theological formulation, a set of laws, or even a prayer form, it certainly did not begin with a document. It began with a person. Christianity is all about commitment to a person. The person of Jesus Christ. Jesus says, Here I am, I stand at the door and knock, if anyone hears my voice and opens the door, I will come in."

"The act of commitment is a prayer of self-offering, which in simple terms expresses belief in Christ as Savior and Lord, acknowledges our sinfulness and need and clearly places our entire life in the hands of Jesus." CRHP Manual

The CRHP manual goes on to say this *"Being a follower of Jesus is not a matter of birth, but of decision. ...The tradition of infant baptism claims the faith of the community for the infant but expects each individual to choose Jesus for himself when he is able to do so."*

How do we do this? How do we choose Him? We must seek Him purposely, intentionally. When we take this step and learn about His love for us, we are choosing to accept Him as our Lord and Savior. This is not an option; it is imperative, a matter of life and death. We have to decide to let Jesus lead our lives. Our lives need to be centered on Jesus. We start a new life in Him. We make the decision to leave our old beliefs, the way we thought about the Ten Commandments, and how we were going to earn our way to Heaven. We decide to grow and mature in our faith and in our relationship with Jesus.

In this new life, we come to realize and accept that we no longer need to earn our way to Heaven. We no longer have to save ourselves, because we have received Jesus' gift of salvation. We accept that He did it all already. He died for and took our sins away from us. He forgave our past, present, and future sins so that we can have access to eternal life. We now have the assurance that we are free. We can now walk in freedom and peace, knowing and truly believing that He rescued us from condemnation. Jesus came to die as a sacrifice for our sins. He made us clean in the eyes of God, the Father. Jesus took all our sins as His own and paid the price for them with His own death. He earned our way to Heaven. We can't earn it, but Jesus earned it for us.

In our previous way of living and thinking, we were uncertain of our future after we died. We thought that we had to earn our way to Heaven by the amount of good deeds we could accomplish. Now, that our relationship with Christ has matured and deepen, we learn how Jesus wants us to live and follow Him. Works are important. It's not enough to just decide to live for Christ. You will start looking like Jesus, and sounding like Jesus, and acting like Jesus.

James 2:18 says, *"Faith without works is dead."*

Even though in this journey we are going to fail at times, and choose to sin, the good news is that when we realize it, we can quickly change, we can turn back and follow Jesus. The deeper our relationship with Jesus becomes, the quicker we realize when we are sinning and then repent immediately. We do this not because we are afraid of Him, not to earn our way to Heaven, or to look good, but because we just hurt our God! We have dishonored Him, and we don't want to disappoint Him. We repent, not because we are afraid of judgment or condemnation, but just because we love Him, and we feel bad that we have failed Him.

When we quickly repent, we are confident in His unconditional love and forgiveness. What Father wants his child to be afraid of him? We want our children to want to do good, not because they are afraid of us, but because they love us and want to honor us. In this new life, our goal is progress, not perfection! We live our lives and spend our time worshiping and loving Jesus. He condensed the 10 commandments into 2 and expanded them to cover much more.

1.   You shall love your God with all your heart, with all your soul, with all your mind, and with all your strength.
2.   You shall love your neighbor as yourself.

In our new life we follow His two commandments to show Him that we Love Him, that we are grateful to Him for what He did and what He does for us and to Honor Him. We do this because we belong to Him and because we are His children.

John 1:10-12 *He came into the very world He created, but the world didn't recognize Him. He came to His own people, and even they rejected Him. But, to all who believed Him and accepted Him, He gave the right to become children of God.*

Written by: Maria Chladny

Article 2 of the Catechism on Justification

1989
The first work of the grace of the Holy Spirit is conversion, effecting justification in accordance with Jesus' proclamation at the beginning of the Gospel: "Repent, for the kingdom of heaven is at hand."[38] Moved by grace, man turns toward God and away from sin, thus accepting forgiveness and righteousness from on high. "Justification is not only the remission of sins, but also the sanctification and renewal of the interior man."[39]

1990
Justification detaches man from sin which contradicts the love of God and purifies his heart of sin. Justification follows upon God's merciful initiative of offering forgiveness. It reconciles man with God. It frees from the enslavement to sin, and it heals.

1991
Justification is at the same time the acceptance of God's righteousness through faith in Jesus Christ. Righteousness (or "justice") here means the rectitude of divine love. With justification, faith, hope, and charity are poured into our hearts, and obedience to the divine will is granted us.

1992
Justification has been merited for us by the Passion of Christ who offered himself on the

cross as a living victim, holy and pleasing to God, and whose blood has become the instrument of atonement for the sins of all men. Justification is conferred in Baptism, the sacrament of faith. It conforms us to the righteousness of God, who makes us inwardly just by the power of his mercy. Its purpose is the glory of God and of Christ, and the gift of eternal life:40

But now the righteousness of God has been manifested apart from law, although the law and the prophets bear witness to it, the righteousness of God through faith in Jesus Christ for all who believe. For there is no distinction: since all have sinned and fall short of the glory of God, they are justified by his grace as a gift, through the redemption which is in Christ Jesus, whom God put forward as an expiation by his blood, to be received by faith. This was to show God's righteousness, because in his divine forbearance he had passed over former sins; it was to prove at the present time that he himself is righteous and that he justifies him who has faith in Jesus.   41 The United States Conference on Catholic Bishops - see http://www.usccb.org/catechism/text/pt3sect1chpt3art2.shtml#35

"Justified through faith", we hear it and continually try to understand it. We want to be made right with and before God. Many of us desire to know God better, to serve Him, and to become right with Him, to become connected with Him. We seek His righteousness. We seek to be made right with Him. We all sin and need to be forgiven and made right with God.

But how do we get there? For centuries in the Old Testament, the only way was through good works, following the rules and laws. Christ came to change all that. Paul comes right to the point in **Romans 1:17**, *"The person who is put right with God (justified and saved) through faith shall live (have eternal life)" (Parenthesis are mine). Good works by themselves do not buy our way into heaven, nor do the*y always reflect what is really in our hearts (Don't we all do good things sometimes for selfish reasons?). Rather, good works are a natural outcome of our faith in God and our desire to please him.

James 2:22 is referring to Abraham when he says, *"…You see that faith was active along with his works, and faith was completed by the works."* Abraham believed in God, and his promises, and therefore was able to act according to God's plan. We all desire salvation but doing good deeds alone will not guarantee it.

Salvation is a free gift of grace, accepted by faith.

James 2:22 is like a plant. Faith can be thought of as the root or the beginning. Hope is the stem, through which the plant is nourished and grows. Love is the flower, the visible result.   We start with **faith** in God, and in his son Jesus Christ, we have **hope** from his promises, and resurrection and we then have **love** for God, and each other, which allows us to do good works for our brothers and sisters.

As humans, we all sin, and our sins have consequences that must be dealt with. God is aware of all of our sins and offers forgiveness through the death of His Son on the cross. We can either accept God's gift of salvation through FAITH IN HIS SON, or we can reject this gift of salvation and suffer God's ultimate judgment. The choice is ours to make. God desires we all accept and receive His forgiveness. As Catholics, we have the opportunity to receive grace and forgiveness in the Sacrament of Reconciliation.

Written by Kate Johnston

Justification, Theology of

The process of a sinner becoming justified or made right with God, as defined by the Council of Trent. "Justification is the change from the condition in which a person is born as a child of the first Adam into a state of grace and adoption among the children of God through the Second Adam, Jesus Christ our Savior" (Denzinger 1524). On "one hand", justification is a true removal of sin, and not merely having one's sins ignored or no longer held against the sinner by God. On "the other hand", it is the supernatural sanctification and renewal of a person who thus becomes holy and pleasing to God and an heir of heaven.

The Catholic Church identifies five elements of justification, which collectively define its full meaning. The primary purpose of justification is the honor of God and of Christ; its secondary purpose is the eternal life of mankind. The main efficient cause or agent is the mercy of God; the main instrumental cause is the sacrament of baptism, which is called the "sacrament of faith" to spell out the necessity of faith for salvation. And that which constitutes justification, or its essence, is the justice of God, "not by which He is just Himself, but by which He makes us just," namely sanctifying grace.

Depending on the sins from which a person is to be delivered, there are different kinds of justification. An infant is justified by baptism and the faith of the one who requests or confers the sacrament. Adults are justified for the first time either by personal faith, sorrow for sin and baptism, or by the perfect love of God, which is at least an implicit baptism of desire. Adults who have sinned gravely after being justified can receive justification by sacramental absolution or perfect contrition for their sins.

Modern Catholic Dictionary by Fr. John A. Hardon, S.J.

NOTES

FAITH WEEK 5   Supernatural Faith

Put on then, as God's chosen ones, holy and beloved, heartfelt compassion, kindness, humility, gentleness, and patience, bearing with one another and forgiving one another, if one has a grievance against another; as the Lord has forgiven you, so must you also do. And over all these put on love, that is, the bond of perfection. And let the peace of Christ control your hearts, the peace into which you were also called in one body. **Col 3:12-15**

✦➤✦

Lord today as one of your chosen ones, I am putting on as my clothing heartfelt compassion, kindness, humility, gentleness and patience. I thank you that I am holy and beloved in your eyes. I choose today to bear with my brothers and sisters, neighbors and friends, forgiving them as the Lord has forgiven me. Today I put on Love and I am letting Christ control my heart with His peace.

DAY 1

READ   Matthew 8: 5-13   The Healing of the Centurion's Servant

1.   What do you think the Centurion means by what he says in vv 8-9?

2.   Jesus is amazed at this Centurion. Why? What does he do that is so amazing to Jesus?

3.   Jesus said, "It will be done for you just as you believed it would." Does this challenge you to believe bigger?

4.   What do we learn about the power of the Word. (See Matthew 8:16; John 1:1, 14; Isaiah 55:11, Genesis 1:1-4)

DAY 2

READ   Matthew15: 1-20

1.   What does Jesus have to say about honoring our parents?

2.   What is unclean according to Jesus? (see verses 10-20)   COMMENT.

God's word is full of advice. God knows what we need, and He has given us the prescription for good health. Proverbs 17:22 tells us a cheerful heart is good medicine, and a broken spirit dries up the bones.

How does our heart become bitter? The root of bitterness lies in unforgiveness. What are we holding onto, meditating on: a failed relationship, our finances, disappointment in a job, not getting the promotion, our marriages, being single? There is a whole host of things that can discourage us. Perhaps the real problem is we are unhappy with ourselves and the choices we have made. We have all made bad choices. We must get past the past.

Yesterday is over. Today is a new day. Refuse to look in the rearview mirror. Instead, look at the beautiful wide-open road ahead. Make the choice today to forgive all the people who have hurt you even if you do not feel it. Say to yourself, "in the name of Jesus, I choose to forgive so and so." Keep saying it until God gives you the grace to forgive that person. Romans 12:2 says to be transformed by the renewing of your mind.

How do we receive that cheerful heart that leads to good health? Set a pattern in your mind to think and meditate on love, joy, peace, and excellent things. Make a commitment to rid yourself of bitterness and unforgiveness and walk in the love of God for yourself and others. Stop your mind from negative thoughts by repeating the name of Jesus each time negativity raises its ugly head. Praise God. Praise is a weapon that drives out anxiety, depression, and fear, which block us from complete joy in Christ. Listen to Christian music, read and memorize scripture and, of course, pray and praise the Lord. Practice these things, and your heart WILL become cheerful, your spirit WILL soar, your face WILL carry a smile, and you WILL be filled with the love of Christ. God wants you healthy and prospering in every area of your life.

Beloved, I hope you are prospering in every respect and are in good health, just as your soul is prospering. **3 John 1:2**

Written by: Lorraine Eastman

DAY 3

READ Mark 11:20-25

1. Is Jesus suggesting we, too, have power over the physical elements? Comment.

2. Do our words have power? Comment. (See Numbers 14:26-30)

3. Describe the faith Jesus is talking about in Mark 11: 23-24

4. Jesus is serious about forgiveness (see Mark 11: 24-25). Please comment. (See also Colossians 3:13 Matthew 6:9-15)

Reflection

Do you have "mountain moving" faith? Do you want it? God says it is in us and even on our lips. How do you speak? Do you say "I can't, I hate, why me, I hate my life, nothing is ever right, nothing ever goes my way, I am the worst, I will never, it figures, here we go again, I am sick of, I am tired of, I am going to die, I feel, and on and on?" When we speak like that, we are full of doubt, fear, and worry.

Instead, we should say…

"I am well,
I am confident,
I am trusting God,
I know I can,
I will prevail,
I am more than a conqueror through Christ,
I can do all things through Christ who strengthens me,
He is my rock,
He will never leave me,
I am a child of the KING OF KINGS, and that makes me a princess/prince.
My God hears my prayers, the prayers of His beloved daughter/son."

"The Lord is with me; I am not afraid; what can mortals do against me." **Psalm 118:6**

Speak to your situation. Say to that mountain….

"Move and go throw yourself in the sea.
My body is well, in the name of Jesus.
I am going to live because I prayed, and I believe in my Lord to heal me.
My sickness, as well as my sins, are on the cross.
My children will return to the Lord.
My husband will get a job because I am trusting in Jesus.
My marriage will be saved because Jesus is my Lord and
He can and will take care of it."

I shall not die but live and declare the deeds of the Lord. **Psalm 118:17**

Why not? We are quick to say the opposite, "I am going to die, I am so sick, my marriage is over… etc." Let's try it, let's start speaking victory, the victory that we have in Christ who died taking all our sins and sicknesses with Him on the cross (Matt 8:17).

DAY 4   READ   James 3:1-12 Power of the Tongue

1.   Describe the power words have. (See Proverbs 18:20-21 and Matthew 12:36)

2.   Describe the tongue and what it does to us.

3.   Recall a time you have said something and regretted it. How did it make you feel? How about the person you said it to? (see Psalm 34:14 NAB)

READ   Proverbs 8:6-8 and 18:20-21

4.   How do these passages encourage you? What does it say to you?

5.   Think of a time when you blessed someone, when you used your words to bring life. How did it make you feel? What was the response from the person? If you can't think of one or one is not coming to you, go and try it. Be deliberate. Speak words of life intentionally today and see what they do.

DAY 5

READ   1 Corinthians 1:18-31

1.   What is the message of the cross?

2. Describe wisdom and foolishness in the following table. (See 1 Corinthians 1:18-31, James 3:17, James 3:13-14 and 1 Corinthians 2:6-7 in table below)

True Wisdom of God	Foolishness of the world
1 Corinthians 1:18-31	1 Corinthians 1:18-31
James 3:17	James 3:17
James 3:13-16	James 3:13-16
1 Corinthians 2:6-7	1 Corinthians 2:6-7

DAY 6

READ the Reflection below

1. Comment about something you learned or found enlightening.

Reflection

Power of Words

Excerpts from Teaching on <u>The Power of the Tongue by Pam Criss,</u> Women's CHRP Retreat, March 7/8, 2009

Who among us has not said something that the moment we spoke the words we want to hit the rewind button and take the words back, reel them back in? But life does not have a rewind button, except maybe in our minds, where we replay misspoken words over and over.

The tongue is a mighty muscle, frequently appearing as the strongest muscle in the body. There are some excellent analogies to explain the power of the tongue in James Chapter 3.

It says: *"If we put bits into the mouths of horses to make them obey us, we also guide their whole bodies. It is the same with ships: even though they are so large and driven by fierce winds, they are steered by a very small rudder wherever the pilots' inclination wishes. In the same way the tongue is a small member and yet has many great pretensions. Consider how small a fire can set a huge forest ablaze. The tongue is also a fire. It exists among our members as a world of malice, defiling the whole body and setting the entire course of our lives on fire, itself on fire by Gehenna."* **(James 3:3-6)**

Think of things that have happened over what SOMEONE SAID; spirits have been crushed, suicides committed, terrorists recruited, people fired, churches left, and relationships severed. Our words are <very> powerful.

> **Proverbs 18:21** *"Death and life are in the power of the tongue; those who make it a friend shall eat its fruit."*

Recently my 14-year-old son spoke at the National Junior Honor Society induction ceremony. I had been studying during that week about the Power of Words so you think I would have had all the right things to say that evening. Not so. He came up to me after the ceremony looking very proud and relieved that it was over, and I blurted out "you weren't loud enough." "Sorry, Mom," he said, "I'm not a good public speaker." Beth Olson, a mom whose daughter was also there that evening and who is a member at St. Gabriel's called me out on the comment, "how about just saying, "Good job, Tyler," she said to me. Oh, she was right! Wait, hit the rewind button! "You are a good speaker, Honey, you did great job." Too late, the damage was done.

As wives, mothers, daughters, co-workers and friends, our words can speak life or speak death; they can build a person up, or tear them down. But how do we train the tongue? How do we learn to speak life and speak LOVE?

First of all, we should do what Jesus did. Jesus always knew the right words to say. We can think of many things that Jesus said that were so profound, so right on. For example, in response to the woman who committed adultery in **John chapter 8 verse 7,** Jesus says, *"Let the one among you who is without sin be the first to throw a stone at her."* And, of course, **John 13 verse 34 & 35:** *"I give you a new commandment: love one another. As I have loved you, so you also should love another. This is how all will know that you are my disciples, if you have love for one another."*

How did Jesus know just what to say?

Every morning before spending time with anyone, Jesus would spend time alone with God. We need to spend time in prayer asking God to show us how to speak. If Jesus needed to be alone with the Father each day before speaking to others, it makes sense that we do too. Very specifically, ask God to guide your words throughout the day. If you're in a situation and you don't know what to say, call on the Holy Spirit at that moment to give you the words. Recall Words of the Bible, strengthen your resolve through prayer, and turn your back on anything that entices you to turn away from God.

Proverbs 12:18 *"The prating of some men is like sword thrusts, but the tongue of the wise is healing."*

A person's day can be turned around by the right words at the right time. A life can be changed by the right words at the right time. Many of us have read the e-mail story about the teenager who was on his way home from school to kill himself. He had cleaned out his locker so that his parents would not have to when he was gone. He was carrying so many books that he dropped them on the walk home. One of the popular kids in the school stopped and helped him pick up the books and talked to him for about a minute. In those seconds and with those few words, the boy changed his mind and decided not to take his life. He went on to become the Valedictorian of that year's graduating class and shared his story during his speech to the shock of the school, his parents, and the boy who helped him pick up his books.

Proverbs 8:6 *"Give heed! For noble things I speak; honesty opens my lips."*

I was at my 7-year old's baseball game last year when a mother was screaming at her son to "HIT THE BALL, SON!" she said over and over. Now, seriously, do you think this little boy standing over home plate did not WANT to hit the ball? Do you think he didn't know he was supposed to hit the ball? The words from the mother were tearing the boy up, not building him up. And no, I wasn't the mom saying these things this time.

Psalm 34:14 *"Keep your tongue from evil, your lips from speaking lies."*

The devil is always tempting us to spread rumors, participate in gossip, say something mean to our husbands, and criticize our children. We have the opportunity with every person we meet and every word we speak to build up the Kingdom of God or tear it down. When the waitress doesn't get the order right, we can criticize and complain, or show her love and compassion. And sometimes the best thing to do is SAY NOTHING AT ALL.

One of the things I always say to my children is "did your mother not teach you, if you don't have anything nice to say, just don't say anything?"

The spiritual mouth exhorts and edifies, it does not criticize. It magnifies strong points in others, not weakness. We all know someone whose mouth is trained to be spiritual. The person can make you feel better in a few minutes of being in their presence. One of the moms I knew through my son's school, Connie McGillen, was that type of person. I attended Connie's funeral last weekend because after 6 years she lost her battle to cancer. As so often happens, once Connie was gone, every conversation I ever had with her became that much more important to me.

And as I was thinking about her, I realized that Connie never spoke ill of anyone, and that she was always very positive and encouraging. She frequently spoke of her faith and always had something nice to say about her husband and sons. She could make you feel welcome and accepted within moments of being with her. Connie knew she was dying, yet she spoke words of life and love at every encounter of every day. She truly had a spiritual tongue.

Let's all learn from Connie and work to train our tongues. If you hear someone talking about someone else, be the person who puts out the fire rather than adding fuel to it. And do it in such a way as to not embarrass those with whom you are talking. Be life-givers with our words, not death givers. Say nice things and learn to listen. God gave us two ears and one mouth, so He must have meant for us to do twice as much listening as talking.

Think of how different our world would look today if we all spoke love. If our tongues were trained and our words guided by the Spirit. I believe we would rarely, if ever, feel the need to hit that rewind button.

Written by: Pam Criss

NOTES

FAITH WEEK 6   Life-Giving Bread

Lord fill me with the knowledge of your will through all spiritual wisdom and understanding. I want to live in a manner worthy of you Lord, and I want to be fully pleasing to you bearing fruit and growing in knowledge of you Lord. Because of your glorious might I am strengthened with power.

DAY 1

READ   Matthew 14: 13-21   Feeding of the Five Thousand

1. Has God ever multiplied anything for you miraculously? If not do you believe it's possible? List a few things God might multiply for us.

2. What does Jesus do before giving the bread to the people? (see John 6:11, Matt 26:26-27)

READ   2 Kings 4:42-44

3. Comment on the multiplication of barley loaves in these verses.

READ   Psalm 37:25 and Matthew 6:11

4. What do these scripture passages say to us and our families? What does God promise us?

Multiplication of the Loaves and Fishes

When we think of multiplying, we usually think of things, i.e., clothes, paper, books, things we have and need or want more of. But there's much more that can be multiplied: love, patience, motivation, understanding, space, time--the intangible things. In Matthew 14 Jesus took what they had, five loaves and two fish and fed the multitudes with it. God doesn't need much to work a miracle, He will work with what you have. God created the universe with just word. God takes what we have and increases it one, two, or a hundred-fold. In His hands anything is possible; the sky is the limit. He is the master multiplier, the king of the universe, creator of all, the ultimate multiplication wiz.

A few weeks ago, I had an experience where God multiplied time for me. I had been out of town and then was home for a few days and had lists to get done before I headed out of town again to dive into plans for our daughter's wedding. I had a full day ahead and asked God specifically to help me get to all my appointments, get all my errands done, and stay with me all day. (And do all this without a speeding ticket or getting stressed out.)

It started with a reminder that our Thursday morning prayer group was meeting at 9 am. I had forgotten it was 9:00 am. I called one of the other gals to see if we were still meeting. She answered and said she couldn't go but told me to go, since they might start later than 9 am. I grabbed by bag, ran to the car, and made it on time. Yes, they had started a bit late that day. After prayer I drove to Plano to pick up something for the wedding that needed to travel with me, and then stopped back at home to freshen up. (Since I had run out at 9 am, I wasn't really ready for the rest of my day.

I proceeded to meet a friend for a relaxing and delicious lunch, and then hit Bed, Bath & Beyond for a gift for a bridal shower that I would be missing, and I wanted to drop it off before I left town. (Yes, I even found my BB&B coupon in the car!) I arrived early (for the first time ever) for my dental appointment that afternoon, dropped the gift off at the bridal shower house and headed home to meet the HV/AC service man to adjust something in our master BR unit. (Had time to make the bed, remember I ran out to prayer that morning.) I did all that with no speeding tickets, stress free, and totally productive. I had started with prayer and praise, asked for help, and then felt the power of His grace with me all day.

Through the obstacles and challenges, God had multiplied my time that day and let me feel His presence in my life. And for that I am most thankful. He is there for us in so many ways that are beyond our comprehension. Ask Him to multiply for you anything you need. We can start today with faith. John 14:14 "If you ask for anything in my name, I will do it."

Written by: Kate Johnston

DAY 2

Moses is God's messenger, mediator, leader, judge, teacher and prophet and he is God's instrument in delivering the Israelite nation from slavery in Egypt where they were enslaved for over 400 years. God leads them out of Egypt and into the promised land and on the way through the desert and wilderness, God feeds His people Manna from heaven every day. God will not let His people starve.

READ   Exodus 16:1-15

1.　Where were the Israelites?

2.　Why were the Israelites complaining and who were they complaining against?

3.　Why did God send manna? (See also Deuteronomy 8:3)

READ   Exodus 16:16-35

4.　Describe the Manna.

5.　What did God instruct them to do regarding the "Manna" and why?

6.　Comment on something you learned.

DAY 3

READ   John 6: 25-40

1.   What kind of food does Jesus want us to work for and where can we get it.?

2.   How does Jesus answer the question, "What are the works of God?" (See verses John 6:28-29)

3.   What is the True bread from heaven?

4.   What does Jesus promise those who come to Him and to those who believe in Him? (see verse John 6:35)

5.   What is the will of God?

6.   Jesus wants everyone to know that He did not come on His own, but that He and the Father are one. In this passage Jesus connects himself to the Father and His Father's work. List every instance. (See also John 5:17)

DAY 4

READ John 6: 41-59

1.   Jesus declares I am.... three times. What does He declare and what is Jesus saying to us?

I am_____

I am_____

I am_____

Jesus says in other places, "I am." Record them here

John 8:58   I am_____

John 9:5   I am_____

John 10:10 I am_____

John 14:6   I am_____

Revelation 1:8 I am _____

2.   Who sent Jesus? Wy is this important to know (John 5:36-37)?

3.   What is Jesus saying about Himself and His Father (See verses John 6:43-46, also verse John 6:57, John 5:19-23,30)

John 6:43-46	
John 6:57	

John 5:19	
John 5:20	
John 5:21	
John 5:22	
John 5:23	
John 5:30	

4.   How do we come to Jesus (See verses John 6:44-47, John 6:64-65)

5.   How do we receive this eternal life that Jesus offers? (See John 6:53-58)

6.   How does Jesus compare Himself to Manna? (See verses John 6: 49,50 and 58)

7.   What does Jesus mean in John 6:45?   See also Jeremiah 31:33-34 and Isaiah 54:13

DAY 5

READ   John 6: 52-59

(John 6:52- 56), The Jews quarreled among themselves saying, "How can this man give us (his)

flesh to eat?" Jesus said to them, "Amen, amen, I say to you, unless you _____ the flesh

of the Son of Man and_____ his blood, you do not have _____ within

you. Whoever_____ my_____ and _____ my _____ has

_____ _____ , and I will raise him on the last day. For my _____ is

_____ food, and my _____ is _____ drink. Whoever _____ my _____

and _____ my _____ remains in _____ and I in _____.

---

1.   Fill out Passage above. What does Jesus promise those who eat His flesh and drink His blood?

DAY 6

1.   How does the loaves and fishes story, Manna, and Jesus' body and blood all relate?

READ John 6:60-65

Comment.

READ   Reflection

2.   Comment about something you learned or found enlightening.

Reflection

Bottom line is that God desires a relationship with us, His creation, and He offers to do the greater share in sustaining that relationship. All we have to do is humbly and reverently accept His gift of life, acknowledging our dependence on Him.

Adam and Eve had wanted for nothing in the garden. They walked with God 'in the cool of the evening'. This is the ideal; but our first parents, in their pride, told God, 'No', essentially, 'I can do this myself' and it has been a long journey back ever since. But God didn't abandon us with a 'Sorry, you guys blew it. I'll be waiting here when you figure it out.' No, He has guided and sustained His people through all the generations of salvation history.

The 40 years the Israelites spent in the desert were a kind of boot camp, a retreat, a workshop, however you want to think about it. Get away from the distractions; get down to the basics; learn discipline; learn ritual; learn reliance on God. If you gather manna according to these rules you will not go hungry. No trying to beat the system by storing it up unless when directed to do so for the Sabbath. Why is this so hard for us to understand? Why do we spend so much time and energy looking for a newer, better and more efficient way? We are to pray, 'Give us this day our daily bread', not 'Stock the pantry. We'll take what we want when we want it and we'll let you know when we are getting low on something.' Trust that God knows what, how much, and when we need to be fed. We are to check in daily, or better yet, pray without ceasing.

And what about those multitudes fed by a few loaves and fishes? Some have pointed out that surely the women at least would have packed a few snacks to keep the kids quiet, but one way or another, at the end of the day, there was more food left over than they started out with and that is a miracle. What is so difficult about believing that the creator of the universe created a little more? The fact is that the people went out for the day not knowing when dinner was going to be served and God/ Jesus took care of their physical, as well as spiritual, hunger. This is a common thread in all the stories we are looking at this week. God uses the elements common to our human experience to demonstrate the elements of His eternal existence. He didn't disdain to take on our human nature for this relationship. He lived among us, died for us and offers us His incarnate self as real food. No, we are not given a faith that is just an exercise for our heads. We are in no uncertain terms directed to eat our Lord's very flesh and drink His blood in order to have life, to feed on Him, to take Him into ourselves so that He can live in us and we in Him. Those that know Greek have said that Luke here used a term for 'eat' that means 'to gnaw' or 'to chew', not merely consume.

Bread and wine, we can understand, but real flesh and blood? That goes against our sensibilities.

Some disciples walked away. Free food and entertainment are great, but when they start asking you to make a commitment, it is time to leave. But Jesus didn't chase after them to explain that He was only speaking figuratively. He meant it literally! Why? It goes back to the Exodus Passover directives. The Hebrew people, in order to be protected from the tenth plague, so that the angel of death would pass over them, were to put the blood of the lamb on the lintels and door posts of their houses (Think of that next time you put the communion cup to your lips.) and eat the roasted flesh of the lamb in community. The old prefigures the new. In the new covenant, we simply <u>must</u> eat the flesh of the sacrificial lamb of God, Jesus, so that death will pass us by and we will have life, eternal life. It is our bread for the journey, our greatest source of grace.

And another thing about blood. Many ancient cultures saw blood as life. An animal's spirit resided in its blood. Drinking an animal's blood was thought to give you the spirit, the strength or other positive traits of that animal. That is precisely why we are <u>not</u> to drink blood. We are not to take on the spirits of animals. Animals are of a lower nature than us humans. But this is God. We <u>want</u> to take into ourselves His Spirit, to take on His nature, to have a share in His divine life, so drink up. His blood is His most intimate gift of His divine self, the gift of a God who desires a relationship with us and offers us a share in His divine work if we would only accept it.

Written by: Joanne Engelke

⤜ ⬦ ⤛

NOTES

FAITH WEEK 7   Covenant

"Let the word of God dwell in you richly" Come Holy Spirit, let the word of God dwell in us richly this week as we study your word. May we become one with you. ***Colossians 3:15***

Feast days in the Old Testament were to be honored. They were sacred assemblies established by God and they were to be kept. They were to be celebrated annually. They were perpetual statutes to be celebrated with fasting, prayer, and accompanied with sacrifice and offerings. These were not your ordinary parties as we know feasts today; they were everlasting ordinances. No one was to work. These feasts were held in honor of our God whom the people believed in and counted on for the harvest, water, for life itself.

We are going to begin this week with a look at the Feast of Passover. Passover is a result of the last plague against the Egyptians. God is calling Pharaoh to release His people. God means business and when Pharaoh refuses, God sends the plagues. Finally, God says every firstborn son in Egypt will die. To read further about the final plague: (Exodus 11:1-7).

DAY 1

READ   Exodus 12:1-30

1.   What does the Lord command the Israelites to do with the lambs on the night of the Passover?

2.   What did the Lord do that night to the Egyptians? (See Exodus 11:4-5 and Exodus 12:23, Exodus 12:29-30)

3.   To the Israelites?

4.   What are the Israelites to do in the future?

5. What does the Passover mean or commemorate? See verse 12:27 (For more information see Notes on Luke 22:15, and on Mark 14:1 in the NAB Bible)

RE - READ Exodus 12:1-13 The Passover meal

6. What is the significance of the Lamb and its blood?

7. Why does God want the Israelites to observe this ceremony year after year?

DAY 2

READ Exodus 19:1-8

1. Where are the Israelites?

2. What is God calling the Israelites to be to him?

3. What was the Israelites response to God?

DAY 3

READ Exodus 23:20-end God is entering into a Covenant with Israel through Moses, referred to as the Mosaic Covenant.

1. What does God promise the Israelites? Write down as many as you can.

2.   Who was this angel and what was his job? (See Exodus 14:19, Ex 32:34, Ex 33:2-3)

READ   Exodus 24:1-12

3.   What was the role of Israel in the Covenant and how do they respond?

4.   How did Moses seal the Covenant?

5.   What happens in verses 9-11 and what does this remind you of?

DAY 4

READ   Luke 22: 1-13

1.   What feast did Jesus celebrate with His apostles? (It is known by two names)

2.   What is the role of the Chief Priests in bringing about the New Covenant?

READ   Luke 22:14-20 This is where the Old Covenant meets Jesus head on

3.   How is God sealing the New Covenant. (See Exodus 24:8)

4.   Why is Jesus referred to as the Paschal Lamb?

5.   What is established here as Covenant?

6.   Comment on the Last Supper and its significance.

READ Hebrews 8:6-13

7.   What does it say about the Old Covenant?

8.   Why is the Old Covenant obsolete

DAY 5

1. What did the shed blood accomplish? Enter answers in the table to the right of each passage.

Leviticus 1:1-4	
Leviticus 17:11	
Hebrews 9:22	

READ   Romans 6:23

2.   What does "wages" mean?

3.   What is the cost of sin? (See Romans 5:12, James 1:15)

4.   What does God require as payment for sin?

5.   Why did blood have to be shed?

Sin cost Jesus His life. He gave it up willingly because of His love for us. Your sin cost Jesus His life. He gave it up willingly because of His love for YOU. If you were the only person alive on earth, God would have sent His son to die in your place. God sent His son Jesus to die for you and instead of you. That is how much He loves you; He gave his son as a ransom for you. He gave His Son for you because you are worth it. To Him, you are worth every drop of blood shed. Jesus shed it all; He gave it all.

Jesus held nothing back. He held nothing back from us, and His desire is that we hold nothing back from him. Since it cost Jesus, everything, don't you think we should let Him take it. Why do we hold onto sin and shame and guilt when He took it away from us and took the punishment for us? He left us free and clear, healed and stainless, alive and clean, forever and ever. As far as the east is from the west, that is how far our sins are from us (Psalm 103:12). That is how truly free and clear we are. He has washed us as white as snow…

Isaiah 1:18 *"Come now, let's settle this,"says the Lord. "Though your sins are like scarlet, I will make them as white as snow. Though they are red like crimson, I will make them as white as wool.*

He doesn't even remember our sins. **Isaiah 43:25** *"I—yes, I alone—will blot out your sins for my own sake and will never think of them again."* Therefore why do we let our sins or sinfulness keep us away from God? He knows when we sin. We cannot hide. He paid not only for your past sins, but your current sins so hurry up and repent and go on. Don't linger and waste away and be pulled down by remembering past sins. Don't stay in the courtroom and listen to the accuser when you have been forgiven and set free. Forgive yourself and be free. Jesus paid a high price for your freedom. Don't remain in prison. He sees you and wants you and knows you are weak; He even knows you will sin again. Still, He died for you.

Isaiah 44:22
I have swept away your sins like a cloud. I have scattered your offenses like the morning mist. Oh, return to me, for I have paid the price to set you free."

Isaiah 53:5
But He was pierced for our rebellion, crushed for our sins. He was beaten so we could be whole. He was whipped so we could be healed.

DAY 6

1.   How do we participate in the New Covenant? Answer in the table below for each verse.

1 Corinthians 10:16	
John 6: 27-29	
Hebrews 10:25	
Romans 10:13	
Romans 10:17	
Acts 1:5,8	

READ and reflect on the notes below.

     5.   What did you learn about Passover and the New Covenant?

Reflection

"Passover" Passover was not just a single event in Israel's history.

The significance of Passover is epic and an event/feast that God wanted His people to remember and celebrate year after year. Passover marked the deliverance from Egypt of God's chosen people, and also served as a foreshadowing of Jesus as the Paschal Lamb that would save the world from slavery to sin.

The lambs blood saved the people of Israel from the wrath of God that night in Egypt when the angel of death passed over every home with the blood of the lamb on its door post. Jesus is the lamb of God. His blood covers all who come to Him for salvation. His blood saves us from the wrath of God against sin.

Jesus is the fulfillment of Passover. He is the perfect "Passover Lamb" that was slain for us. The blood of the lamb covered the doorpost, but the blood of Jesus, the LAMB OF God, covers us. It not only covers our sins but wipes them away. The Old Testament Passover is no longer in effect; it has been fulfilled in Christ who delivers His people permanently and effectively and completely from slavery to sin. We as the Church celebrate the Eucharist as our Passover supper. The Lord's supper has replaced the Passover supper. We celebrate Easter each year when we commemorate what Jesus has done for us through His death, burial, and resurrection.

Who but God could change Passover? Passover was the summit and font of the Israelites' faith. And Jesus, at the last Passover meal, ESTABLISHED a NEW covenant. He established himself as God. JESUS IS LORD, HE IS God; who but God could fulfill the old covenant and establish a new and better one? Jesus is the New Covenant, and He is about to establish it with His blood, which He will pour out on the cross. He is the sacrificial lamb, the paschal lamb, the true lamb, the only perfect lamb, the unblemished lamb.

He is the lamb sacrificed for the sins of the people. Jesus was nailed to the cross during Passover; sacrificed to SAVE the people, like the blood of the lamb on the night of Passover. Just like the blood of the lamb applied to the doorposts saved the nation, Jesus saves us with His blood shed for us. His blood is now "applied" to us. He is our savior, the lamb that was slain, the Lamb of God. God chose this perfect lamb for himself. Jesus is not only the Lamb but the High Priest who offers the blood. He offers His very own blood. He not only died for us but intercedes for us at the right hand of God.

New Covenant

Jesus is our lifeline.   He is the bridge between heaven and earth. Through him, we are in a covenant relationship with the Father. He didn't come to give us a set of rules to live by; that was the Old Covenant. Jesus came to make us one with Him and to have a relationship with us. He came to make us His children.

God made a covenant with you.   He didn't have to.

He made us promises, and He has obliged himself to us. He didn't have to. He promised to protect us. He promised to be our God, and He signed this covenant with the Blood of Jesus. He didn't have to. He gave us Himself in the Eucharist that we may partake of this NEW COVENANT. We partake or consume the sacrificial lamb slain for us. He came to bring us life, and He wants us to choose life in him. When we eat this bread and drink this wine, we declare His death and resurrection to the whole world. We let everyone know we believe that He died for our sins and rose to bring us new life.

The Eucharist is our yes to Jesus.

We remind ourselves, those who see us, and even God, that we are believers; we are his. We let the world and the devil know we are born into the KINGDOM of God and do not belong to this world. We are God's very own children. When we partake of the Eucharist, we share in the New Covenant.

We become one with Him and each other. It is our declaration of who we are and who we believe in. When we consume the body of Jesus, we remember the covenant and the sacrifice it took to ratify it. Jesus became one of us and died for us. He represents us, since He is a man and a fellow member of the human race. He had to become one of us to represent us. Yet because He is God, He can be that perfect lamb and rise from the dead, bringing us into a new life.
Just like in the OLD COVENANT or Old Testament, the bulls and lambs were slain to cover the sins of the people. Jesus took the cross to be slaughtered for us once and for always. Forever and ever, He took away our sins, freeing us from the guilt, shame, and bondage of sin.

JEREMIAH 31:31-33

> *"Behold, the days are coming, declares the Lord, when I will make a new covenant with the house of Israel and the house of Judah, ….33 For this is the covenant that I will make with the house of Israel after those days, declares the Lord: I will put my law within them, and I will write it on their hearts. And I will be their God, and they shall be my people."*

When we partake of the sacrament or sacrifice of Christ, we ratify our membership in the new covenant. We confirm who we are. We remind God that we remember what Christ did for us. Every time you take communion, you are saying Yes to Jesus, yes to the Father. Jesus did the work. Jesus did the hard part. Our part is to receive and partake.

The Father chose a Covenant relationship with us through Christ Jesus.

He can't go back on His word and He won't. He can't go back on His word because the spilled blood was permanent. He can't "un-spill" His blood. Even if He could change His mind, He won't. He doesn't want to!

God gets nothing out of His covenant with you except YOU. You, on the other hand, get everything. The Bible says that all of God's promises are *"yes and amen in Christ Jesus, our Lord"* (2 Corinthians 1:20). There is so much more to God than we know. God made a covenant of promises to us through Jesus. There is access to every promise God made, but only through Jesus. He is the way. Jesus made the covenant with God for us and willingly died for us to secure it for us forever. We get it all through Him.

He didn't have to. He chose to make a covenant with us. We can't earn it or work for it. It is ours through a relationship with him. He chose us!! He chose to be one with us in Christ. The Father chose to be our God and through this covenant relationship we get all the benefits. He signed the covenant with the Blood sacrifice of His very own son Jesus Christ.

Jesus became a curse so we could receive all the blessings.

GALATIANS 3:13-14

"Christ ransomed us from the curse of the law by becoming a curse for us, for it is written, "Cursed be everyone who hangs on a tree," that the blessing of Abraham might be extended to the Gentiles through Christ Jesus, so that we might receive the promise of the Spirit through faith."

People are perishing and walking through a hopeless, fruitless life all because they don't know the riches that belong to those who are children of the King. Jesus chose to be cursed so we could inherit the land (the kingdom of God) and be blessed. God bought for us the all-expense-paid trip to eternity. We need to enjoy all the benefits of being a child of the King. These benefits God paid a mighty high price for. He did it because we are worth it to him.

Jesus is everything.

Now you must begin to renew that soul of yours: your mind, your will, and your emotions. Your soul has been trained in the flesh, but now it's time to train your soul in the Spirit. Time to grow up. The Bible says to renew your mind.

Psalm 119:9-11
How can the young keep his way without fault? Only by observing your words. With all my heart I seek you; do not let me stray from your commandments. In my heart I treasure your promise, that I may not sin against you.

We transform ourselves and our minds, our will, and our emotions by reading God's Word and praying in the Holy Spirit.

James 1:21
Therefore, put away all filth and evil excess and humbly welcome the word that has been planted in you and is able to save your souls.

Psalm 119:105
Your word is a lamp for my feet, a light for my path.

Hebrews 4:12
For the word of God is alive and powerful. It is sharper than the sharpest two-edged sword, cutting between soul and spirit, between joint and marrow. It exposes our innermost thoughts and desires.

Stay Grounded in God's word and watch your life be renewed.

NOTES

FAITH WEEK 8   Saving Cup

My children, I am writing this to you so that you may not commit sin. But if anyone does sin, we have an Advocate with the Father, Jesus Christ the righteous one. He is expiation for our sins, and not for our sins only but for those of the whole world.   ***1 John 2:1-2***

DAY 1

READ   Hebrews 7:1-10 and Genesis 14:17-20

1.   Who is Melchizedek and what do we know about him?

2.   What is the significance of the tithe or tenth and Abraham's giving it to Melchizedek?

READ   Malachi 3:6-12

3.   What does God promise those who tithe? What is God saying to us?

DAY 2

READ Hebrews 5:1-6

1.   What does this mean... Jesus is a priest in the order of Melchizedek? (See also Hebrews 7:23-25, 6:19-20)

READ Hebrews 4:14-16

2.   What does Jesus do for us as our High Priest?

READ   Hebrews 7:11-17

3.   Why is it important to know that Jesus is High Priest according to the order of Melchizadek. (See Hebrews 7:21-25)

4.   Hebrews 7:12 is profound; what is it saying?

DAY 3

READ   Hebrews 7:11-28   READ   Hebrews 10:5-18

1.   Write down words or phrases describing each from the scriptures above and list them in the table below.

Old Priest/Priesthood	New Priest/Priesthood in Jesus

2.   What is the difference between the Old Priest/Priesthood and the New Priest/Priesthood?

DAY 4

READ   Hebrews 8

1.   Why did we need a New Covenant; a new and better sacrifice?

READ   Hebrews 9:9-22 and 10:1-4

2.   Why is Jesus' sacrifice so much better?

3.   Why was His death so important?

4.   What do we learn about the blood of the covenant; the blood of the sacrifice; blood in general?

DAY 5

READ   Hebrews 9:1-8, and 23-28   Compare the Sanctuaries!!!

1.   How do the priesthoods differ regarding sanctuaries?

"For He has rescued us from the dominion of darkness and brought us into the kingdom of the Son He loves in whom we have redemption, the forgiveness of sin." **Col. 1:13.**

Jesus paid for our freedom with His blood. Remember hearing or reading about Jesus being tempted in the desert? The devil came to tempt Jesus. The devil came to stop Jesus from saving us. The devil didn't want us free from his control. He wanted to thwart the plan of GOD. He wanted Jesus stained. He wanted Jesus imperfect, so that He could not be "The Lamb." The Unblemished lamb, the spotless lamb.

The devil wants us to remain in bondage, in fear, and worry. Because Jesus was perfect, He was sacrificed for our sins. We have a choice; we can stay in bondage to sin or be set free. It has already been paid for. Say this out loud when confronted by evil, "Jesus is my Lord." Remind the devil to whom you belong. Know today that you are free because His death is true. He paid for your freedom, so be free. You are His.

Written by: Mark Wuenschel

DAY 6

1.   How does Jesus fulfill the old covenant? (See definition of FULFILL - below)

1 Peter 1:18-19	
John 1:29	
Hebrews 9:15	
Romans 13:8	

Fulfill

1. To carry out or bring to realization, as a prophecy or promise
2. To perform or do, as duty; obey or follow, as commands
3. To satisfy (requirements, obligations, etc.): a book that fulfills a long-felt need
   To bring to an end; finish or complete, as a period of time: He felt that life was over when one had fulfilled his threescore years and ten.
   Taken from http://dictionary.reference.com/browse/fulfill

READ Notes on the pages that follow

2.   Comment about something you learned or found enlightening.

Reflection:

HIGH PRIEST   Jesus is not only the Lamb but also the High Priest who offers the blood. In the Old Testament, The High Priest sprinkled the blood on the mercy seat in the Holy of Holies behind the veil each year on the Day of Atonement. The blood of the sacrificed animal "covered" the sins of the people. The mercy seat is the cover of the Ark of Covenant and resides behind the veil in the Holy of Holies. The broken Ten Commandment tablets were in the Ark of Covenant. When God looked down, He did not see the broken tablets or the sins of the people He saw the blood that was sprinkled on the mercy seat (also called Propitiatory). God saw the blood and was satisfied temporarily, and until they sinned again. The High Priest brought the sacrifice, for the nation of Israel, into the Holy of Holies once a year on the Day of Atonement.

NOW, JESUS IS our HIGH PRIEST. He brought the offering to God in the TRUE HOLY OF HOLIES, heaven itself. The tabernacle of the Old Covenant was set up on earth as a copy of the perfect tabernacle in heaven. The blood sacrifices of the Old Testament were a foreshadowing of the Cross. The Cross was the final sacrifice. That is why Jesus said on the Cross, "It is Finished."

Jesus brings the blood (his very own blood) to the very throne room of God. His blood now covers/wipes outs forever the sins of the people!

We are the people. In the First Covenant, God tells Abraham, you will be my people, and I will be your God. Through Jesus WE ARE HIS PEOPLE. From the Nation of Israel to many nations. When God saw the Blood of Jesus, He was satisfied, completely satisfied, forever satisfied. His blood was shed once. He does not have to shed blood again every time we sin. His blood is eternal. Jesus not only died but rose from the dead to destroy death. He destroyed death, that we might live forever in heaven with Jesus. We too, are raised from the dead to new life in him. He died for us and rose for us that we might live, and live forever.

Because HE LIVES, He is our mediator. He is not only the LAMB, and THE HIGH PRIEST of the New Covenant, but also the MEDIATOR of the New Covenant. He now sits at the right hand of the Father, forever interceding for US. Jesus says, *"I am the way, the truth, and the life; no one goes to the Father except by me"* **John 14:6.**

Read Leviticus 16 if you would like to read further about the Day of Atonement; the day the Israelites offered the sacrifice for the sins of the nation.

The Paschal Lamb

Jesus is the Paschal lamb, the Passover lamb. He is called the Passover lamb because He was crucified on Passover, and He is the fulfillment of Passover. He is the sacrificial Lamb sacrificed for us. His death brings us life. Just like the blood of the Passover lamb was spread upon the doorposts of every Israelite family, Jesus' blood covers us. Just like the angel of death passed over every home covered in blood, in Egypt that night before all of Israel was freed from slavery, Jesus saves us from death, all who are covered with the blood of Jesus.

Jesus fulfills Passover because He is the final Lamb. Once He sacrifices His life for us, there is no longer any sacrifice left. He is the true Lamb, the final Lamb, and the forever sacrifice. He sacrificed His life for all sins: past, present, and future.

The Passover meal was celebrated by the Israelites the night before the firstborn child of every Egyptian family was killed. It has been celebrated every year since as a memorial of the saving power of God. The Last Supper (Eucharist), fulfills Passover. Passover is now obsolete because Jesus ended Passover and began the Eucharistic celebration, the night before He died. At the Last Supper, Jesus said, "Do this in memory of me." Do this, Jesus said, and remember how I died to set you free. Now we celebrate this new covenant and will continue until Jesus comes again.

"At the Last Supper, on the night He was betrayed, our Savior instituted the Eucharistic sacrifice of His Body and Blood. This He did in order to perpetuate the sacrifice of the cross throughout the ages until He should come again, and so to entrust to His beloved Spouse, the Church, a memorial of His death and resurrection: a sacrament of love, a sign of unity, a bond of charity, a Paschal banquet 'in which Christ is consumed, the mind is filled with grace, and a pledge of future glory is given to us.'" CCC 1323

CCC 571, The Paschal mystery of Christ's cross and Resurrection stands at the center of the Good News that the apostles, and the Church following them, are to proclaim to the world. God's saving plan was accomplished "once for all"313 by the redemptive death of his Son Jesus Christ.

FOR FURTHER STUDY

You may find the following enlightening!!! You may want to spend time studying this with your family. The Israelites participated in the Old Covenant, through Circumcision, Passover meal, Sacrificial system and the Law.

READ   Luke 24:28-35   The first reenactment of the Lord's Supper
1.   What happened during the meal? What happens when we partake in communion?

READ   1 Corinthians 11:17-34
2.   What does Paul teach us about Eucharist?

3.   When do we stop celebrating the Eucharist?

Covenant:

Covenant is the translation of the Hebrew word Berith, which means testament. The word Berith is used to designate every type of contract or alliance between private individuals, tribes or peoples. It passed over into religious language to signify the historical relationships which God deigned to establish with the people of Israel and with the whole of humanity. The biblical alliance or covenant applied to the relationships between God and man is quite different from the type of accord through negotiation which culminates in a contract between equals, such as happens in business affairs.

Source: The New World Dictionary-Concordance to the New American Bible

NOTES

FAITH WEEK 9   Heroic Faith

The LORD is my light and my salvation; whom do I fear? The LORD is my life's refuge; of whom am I afraid? When evildoers come at me to devour my flesh, these my enemies and foes themselves stumble and fall. Though an army encamp against me, my heart does not fear; Though war be waged against me, even then do I trust. ***Psalm 27:1-3***

DAY 1

READ   1 Samuel 16: 1-13   David and Goliath

1. What is the difference between the way we look at a person and the way the Lord looks at a person? (See 2 Corinthians 5: 6-7, 12, 15, 16) (See 2 Corinthians 10: 7)

2. Does the Lord speak to you like He speaks to Samuel, or does He speak differently to you? How and what kind of things does the Lord talk to you about?

DAY 2

READ   1 Samuel 17: 1-19

According to Webster, the word "defy", means to challenge, to do something considered impossible. The Bible says in verse 10 that Goliath defied the ranks of the Israelites. Goliath is staring them in the face and saying, "I dare you. I dare you to fight me."

1. Why were the Israelites so afraid, so terrified? (see Samuel 17:11)

2. Describe Goliath.

3.　Describe David.

During the time of David and the early Kings, fighting took place mostly hand to hand, sword to sword, knife to knife, etc. Each army stood on the top of their prospective hills with a valley between them on purpose. They could see each other, and they knew when the other army made a move. Since it was such a long way down and then a long, tiring way up the opposite side, it was common to send one person to fight. Each army would send their best warrior.

DAY 3
READ　1 Samuel 17:20-37

1.　What did David mean in verse 26 when he referred to Goliath as "Uncircumcised"?

2.　How does David react/respond to the taunting of his brothers?

3.　What did David say to convince Saul to let him fight Goliath, even though he was only a boy?

4.　Why did Saul let David fight?

DAY 4

READ 1 Samuel 17:38-47

Please read this scripture! Don't miss reading this STORY even if you know the story and have read it before. It will be brand new for you if you read it again now with the Holy Spirit. God has something He wants to tell you today.

1. What did David say to Goliath? Write it out word for word.

2. Why wasn't David afraid of Goliath even when all the other soldiers were terrified? Should he have been afraid? (READ Deuteronomy 20:1-4)

3. How does David react/respond to the taunting of Goliath?

4. In whom did David trust? How do we know that?

5. Do you have a Goliath in your life? Is it time to slay that giant? Who is your ever-present help in time of need?

Finish reading 1 Samuel 17

6. Comment about something you learned or found enlightening.

Notice in verse 45 how David, when confronting Goliath, points out to Goliath that he has defied GOD by coming against the Israelites. David recognizes that Goliath is in deep trouble because he is not making war just on the Israelites, but against God himself. When Goliath insults God's people he is insulting God. Because of this knowledge, that only David seemed to have, David was able to overcome and conquer Goliath and hence, the entire Philistine Army, through the power of the Lord God Almighty in whom he trusted.

David PROCEEDS TO TALK SMACK! "Today the Lord shall deliver you into my hand; I will strike you down and cut off your head. This very day I will leave your corpse and the corpses of the Philistine army for the birds....." You have to know you are going to win to talk like this.

David did everything he said he would do; he even cut off the giant's head! It is time now to cut off the head of the devil speaking lies to us all day long.

DAY 5

READ Ephesians 6: 10–20 Armor of God

1.   Who supplies the armor, and for what purpose?

2.   Describe who our struggle is against and who is it not against?

3.   Goliath had a shield made of iron or bronze and had his shield bearer carry it for him. What kind of shield did David have? What is our shield? And what does it do for us?

4.   What is the sword of the spirit?

5. Memorize the scripture, pray it, teach it to your children. Imagine touching your children and saying, "Joey, draw your strength from the Lord...."

DAY 6

READ 2 Corinthians 10:1-6

1. What does this scripture say?

2. READ Reflection below and comment.

Reflection

David and Goliath is such a great story!
It is a true story and a remarkable, glorious story of victory.

David is just a boy, yet when he comes to where the Israelites are camped, he sizes up the situation instantly, and offers a solution. Here we have two opposing armies lined up for battle on two separate hills with a valley in between. Goliath has been taunting them for weeks now. The Israelites are dismayed and terrified of him and their dismal situation. When they see Goliath each day, the Bible says they run from him in great fear. There is no victory in sight; they are just waiting while hoping for deliverance.

David comes, sees Goliath and says basically, "who is this piece of trash, this man who dares to insult God and His people." When Saul, the King, sends for David after overhearing him, David tells him not to worry about anything. "I will fight this Philistine." "Yeah, right," Saul says, "you are just a boy, and he has been a soldier forever. What can you possibly do?" "Ha," David says (paraphrased), "This is nothing. I have rescued sheep from the mouth of lions and bears. I have killed lions and bears, this 'uncircumcised Philistine' will be like one of them because he has insulted the living God. The Lord has delivered me before, and He will do it again."

DAVID had no doubt whose side God was on. He knew that the Lord would back him up and bring him victory. How did He know? Why was He so sure?

1. Goliath was uncircumcised. Hello! In the wrong army! Nobody messes with God's children. How come it takes so many of us so long to figure that out? The rest of the army must have forgotten. They lived in fear! They were defeated even though God was on their side. They lacked faith in their God, and therefore had no victory. Maybe, just maybe, your lack of victory is due to your lack of faith.

2. David had a relationship with God. He walked and talked with God and wrote songs to God. David hung out with God all day long while tending the sheep. David was God's child, and he KNEW it. Everything that belongs to the Father belongs to His child! When you are a child of the KING OF KINGS, you are a prince/princess. David knew whose he was. David knew to whom he belonged. He didn't wonder, he knew.

3. David had experienced God's deliverance, over and over again. God had come through for him so often, David knew an enemy when he saw one.

4. David had faith. Great faith.

Because David did believe, he wasted no time. His brothers hated him for it and thought he was conceited. They called him arrogant and evil. Good thing he was not easily put off or distracted.

Persevere and don't quit now. The best is yet to come!

Most people do not let others know what they think of them, or will not quickly let on, such as friends, acquaintances, or co-workers. If you are getting on their nerves, they usually take it. They may be saying a lot inside their heads about you, but usually not out loud. "Usually." Then there are those pesky family members like David's brothers. They aren't afraid to tell David what they really think: "who do you think you are, how dare you, you arrogant evil little...."

David lets it roll right off him. He is not even phased by it. He knows who he is. He knows to whom he belongs. He knows who is looking out for him. He knows his deliverer. It is usually those closest to us who hurt us the most. The battle plan is to put on the Armor of God and resist the devil. Remember, it is not them we are fighting but the devil. Be like David, and do not listen to them anymore. Let them say what they will, but we will not listen to the taunts of the enemy.

Battle Plan
Okay, if you didn't have a battle plan, you have one now.

Do you have problems in your life? Are you fighting for your life, for your marriage, for your job, for your children?

The Bible says the devil comes to kill, steal, and destroy. Are we going to sit back and take it, cower like the Israelites? OR do we know who we are, whose we are? If we do know who we are and who we belong to, then let's act like it and talk like it.

David is ready and has a plan, a battle plan. David is ready to fight and not only fight but to go all the way to Victory! Don't give up before the Victory. David said, "you come against me with a sword, a spear, and scimitar, but I come against you in the name of the Lord of hosts, the God of the armies of Israel that you have insulted." David did not let Goliath scare him, move him, or get him nervous. He did not listen to his taunting. Instead, he fought him with the spiritual weapons of warfare.

SAY THIS....

"Devil you are NOT coming between me and my _____ {fill in the blank}. You come against me with lies, insults, foul language, bitterness, but I come against you in the name of Lord of Hosts. Jesus is my Lord, my defender, my hero, my mighty warrior!"

Goliath came against David with his heavy, huge armor. The Bible even tells us how much each piece weighed. He came with a shield-bearer going out in front of him. David went out in the protection of the Lord. The Bible says. God is.... our shield, our armor, our protection, our fortress, our strong tower, our ever-present help in time of need.

David ran to meet the enemy. He didn't wait; he went on the offensive!!! Get up in the morning and speak to your situation. Speak life into your circumstances.

Stop pondering or dwelling on your situation. Get up and fight today and every day until you have the victory. Be on the offense. Is your job weighing you down? Get up and speak as you are getting dressed. I am going to work; I am a soldier for Christ. My boss is a good boss. My day is good because Jesus is my Lord and going with me. I will love my co-workers today. They will feel the presence of God today because I am near. I am successful today. I will excel because Jesus goes before me. I have the favor of God on me. Blessings are chasing after me because I am a child of the most high God.

Victory

Victory is David's! The Victory is ours!

David gives all the glory, all the credit to God!!! David says …. "The whole land will learn that Israel has a God…. All this multitude, too, shall learn that it is not by sword or spear that the Lord saves. For the battle is the Lord's and he shall deliver you into our hands."

NOTES

FAITH WEEK 10   Trust/Humility

The LORD is my light and my salvation— whom shall I fear? The LORD is the stronghold of my life— of whom shall I be afraid? When the wicked advance against me to devour me, it is my enemies and my foes who will stumble and fall. Though an army besiege me, my heart will not fear; though war break out against me, even then I will be confident. **(Ps. 27)**

DAY 1

READ   Matthew 1:18-25 and Luke 1:26-38

1.   Who had faith and how did they show it?   Comment.

READ   Matthew 2:1-12

2.   Who believes and how did they show it? (see also Luke 2:8-20)

DAY 2

READ   Matthew 4:18-22

1.   Imagine that was you. What would you do? OH! It is YOU!

READ   Matthew 9:35-38

2.   What does Jesus want from us and why? Comment.

DAY 3
READ   Psalm 112

1.   Because we trust in the Lord, what is ours, and who are we? What can we expect? Write them all down.

 Remember You are the righteousness of GOD IN CHRIST JESUS. We are the righteous not because we are sinless or never sin, but because we were bought and paid for by the blood of Christ. We live in the age of Forgiveness and renewal in Christ Jesus. We have been born again in Christ. It is not us that lives, but He that lives in us. We are HIDDEN in Christ. He became sin so that we would be set free from sin. We are either free from sin or not. Declare it today; we are set free because Jesus died to set us free. We receive that freedom now in order to glorify the one that sets us free.

He is the reason we are righteous, not our own good works. He makes us righteous, not ourselves. God says in His word, over and over again to forget about the past and move on. We have been forgiven, just because you haven't forgiven yourself doesn't mean God hasn't forgiven you. He is not holding out, waiting until you make it right. There's nothing we can do to make it right. What is done is done, and there is nothing that we can do to undo it. Nothing WE can do, that is. It is done, but GOD does say it can be erased!!! Erased to a white that is whiter than white.

God says there is no memory of it even on His books or in His mind. He says He places our sins so far from him, **Psalm 103:12** says *"as far as the east is from the west, so far has He removed our transgressions from us.*

WHERE TWO OR MORE ARE GATHERED. Maria Chladny and I were trying to remember a certain scripture we had heard during our prayer time at Bible Study. We were searching desperately through Isaiah, trying to remember which chapter we read from earlier that week. Maria remembered the Lord speaking to her in this scripture. It was profound, and she was changed. We looked and looked, and I told her that even when we find it, it will not be the same or speak to us the same way. There is an anointing when we are together, that is special. When we pray and read God's Word together, God is with us and speaks to us. He speaks to us through His Word. It is our manna for that day. The Word of God is alive.

Someone once told me you could read the same scripture verse every day for a month, and God would tell you something different each day. It is true. The Holy Spirit is with you and opens up the Word to you if you invite him.

DAY 4
READ   Matthew 18:1-9, Matthew 19:13-15

1.   Who is greatest in the Kingdom of Heaven?

2.   What does each scripture say about the proud and the humble?

	"PROUD"	"HUMBLE"
1 Peter 5:5-7		
Luke 14:7-11		
James 4:6-10		

	"PROUD"	"HUMBLE"
Psalm 25:9		
Matthew 16:24-27		
Proverbs 18:12		
Proverbs 3:34		

3. Reflect on the scriptures in the table on the previous page. Summarize what you learned about pride and humility.

DAY 5
READ   Romans 12:17-21

1. Comment:

DAY 6
READ   Daniel 4   Story of the humbling of Nebuchadnezzar

1. What happens to Nebuchadnezzar?

2.   What did you learn from this story?

OPTIONAL   READ Acts 12: 19-23

1.   What other King was humbled? How and why?

Imagine a life where God is the center. Your life is lived to please him, glorify and honor Him above all else and above all others including yourself. Imagine your life centered around the will of God. Imagine your life centered around God's concerns, His cares, His feelings, His likes. That is where He is leading us. He is leading us to a God-centered existence because it is the only way to truly live. When God is the center and focus of our lives, we live and are free from all stress and strife. We are not concerned or burdened with our own advancement, honor, and glory. If we are last, He is first. If we put ourselves first, He is usually last. With God, everything is upside down. His ways are not our ways. His ways are not the world's ways. The last shall be first, and the first shall be last. It is in giving that we receive. It is in dying that we are born to eternal life. The meek shall inherit the earth.

When God is center, or first, we are telling the world that we trust Him, that He is worthy of our trust. Our confidence is in Him to come through for us; we don't have to play the world's game. We have a Father who is watching out for us and cares for us, not only in the next life but in THIS life.

Do you want the glory you think you deserve? Do you want the attention or accolades someone else is receiving? God can never be glorified through us if we are glorifying ourselves or seeking the glory that belongs to God and God alone. When we want the recognition, we are not concerned with God receiving the recognition. When I am concerned with how I look to others, I am usually not worried about how God looks. It's either me or Him, and every time I am concerned with ME; I am not thinking about God or how God looks to others.

When we put God first and care more about Him than our feelings, we will always be satisfied. This is a promise from God: "Humble yourself in the sight of the Lord, and He will exalt YOU."

NOTES

FAITH WEEK 11   Walking on Water

Seek the LORD while he may be found; call on him while he is near. Let the wicked forsake their ways and the unrighteous their thoughts. Let them turn to the LORD, and he will have mercy on them, and to our God, for he will freely pardon. **Isaiah 55:6-7**

❧ ◆ ❧

DAY 1

READ Mark 9:14-29   Healing of a Boy with a Demon

1.   Who is Jesus upset with and why?

2.   What is possible for the person with faith? For you?

3.   What does Jesus mean when He says, "if you can?" (See Mark 11:23 24)

4.   When is it hard to believe?

5.   How did Jesus respond to the father's plea? (See Mark 9:19 and 29)

6.   Do you think Jesus is trying to tell us something. Is there a connection?

"I believe Lord, Help me with my unbelief." Mark 9:24 I pray this prayer all the time, especially when I don't have the faith that I know I am lacking. The Bible is full of prayers. It is powerful to pray God's word back to Him. His word is perfect and therefore, so is our prayer when we pray God's Word. I pray this prayer; "I believe Lord, help me with my unbelief," when I know my faith is not where it needs to be for any given situation.

UNBELIEF: Boy with a Demon We all go through times of unbelief, maybe even daily! The good news is that we can turn to God for faith. He is not only the author of our faith but the finisher as well. Jesus is speaking about His disciples again when He mentions their unfaithfulness. Jesus again speaks to the disciples about their lack of faith. JESUS is not afraid to offend them. It is in offending them that they will grow and learn.

When you are offended, praise God, it is an opportunity for you to learn, to grow and to mature. Just like our muscles need to be bruised and torn in order to grow bigger and stronger, so we too, grow painfully sometimes. I will never be satisfied with my level of faith. I want more. I will always have room to grow. Sometimes we are offended by those who say we need more faith, or where is your faith? Do not be offended. Realize that your faith is lacking and run to the source of faith.

We cannot live on our own or have faith on our own. We need Jesus, and we need each other. No one can do this on her/his own. No one. Jesus said to His disciples, "where is your faith"? They lost their faith, over and over again and so do we. We are in good company if we are faithless. Even the disciples of Jesus, those who walked with Him and listened to Him were faithless at times.

The good news is we know where to get more faith and how to get it. Turn to Him, read His word, pray and ask for faith, go to church, and call your friends in Christ. Don't just sit there. Know that you alone are not enough. AND know that it is okay to be faithless, just don't stay there. Do something about it.

Why are the Israelites so faithless? What or who are they listening to, believing? Why were the Israelites so unfaithful? What were they missing? They were missing the Holy Spirit. The apostles were fearful before Pentecost. They sat huddled in the upper room because they were afraid to go out. However, on the day of Pentecost, the disciples were filled with the Holy Spirit, and they were no longer fearful. On that very day, Peter left the upper room and preached to thousands. Three thousand people came to believe in Jesus that day.

I am the vine you are the branches, Jesus says, remain in me. If today you think you have faith, tomorrow's circumstances will prove you wrong. That is why we need to remain in Him. Jesus said, *"If you remain in me and my words remain in you, ask for whatever you want, and it will be done for you.* By this is my Father glorified, that you bear much fruit and become my disciples."

The Father is desperate to have his son healed. He says: "Please if you can do anything." "IF," Jesus says, as if to say, Don't you know who I am?" God is not moved by how desperate we are. God is not moved by our needs, our pain, our plight, our circumstances. Many are desperate. Many are hurting, sick, some are so desperate they resort to dangerous drugs, crime, and unhealthy relationships. If God were moved to heal by our circumstances, or our plights, no one would be in need. Jesus said to the man, *"If you can! EVERYTHING is possible for the one who has faith."* WOW! Everything is available to the one who believes. God responds to faith! The man knew he didn't have it, so he said, "I believe Lord, help me with my unbelief."

DAY 2

READ   John 4:7-42   The Samaritan Woman

1.   What is Jesus offering the woman and us and why? (See John 4:7-15)

2.   How is Jesus fed?

3.   Why did the Samaritans come to hear Jesus? What made them believe in him?

Note: Imagine Jesus is fed as He ministers to us according to the Father's will. Not only is Jesus loving and ministering us, but He thrives on it. It is His very life. Does He not offer the same to us? We think it will cost us to serve and follow and give and lay down our lives but it is just the opposite. We not only live but thrive and succeed and prosper. He is the bread of life.

DAY 3

READ   Matthew 14:23-33   Walking on Water

1.   Why did Peter want to come to Jesus on the water? What made him step out of the boat?

2.   What happens when you step out of the boat?

3.   Are we afraid to step out of the boat? WHY?

4.   What made Peter afraid and what happened when he became afraid?

You have to wonder what it must have felt like to see Jesus walking on the water.........
what it must have felt like to walk on water.

May I suggest that Peter's past had nothing to do with his walking on the water or his sinking, only the present had any bearing on whether or not he sank or walked. Only his faith, trust and obedience in Jesus at that moment. The moment his eyes left Jesus he began to sink.

DAY 4

READ   Matthew 14:23-33 again

1.   What can keep Peter from sinking?

2.   Do we ever sink? Give examples of sinking experiences people face.

3.   How can we keep from sinking today? How do we keep our problems or things that happen to us from stealing our faith or peace?

4.   Jesus asked Peter, "Why did you doubt?"   Does Jesus expect too much from us? COMMENT!

5.   Why did Jesus rescue Peter? What do you learn about Jesus from this?

After Peter fell into the water, how do you think he got back to and into the boat? Do you think Jesus dragged him back to the boat, carried him or do you think maybe he got up and began walking on water with Jesus? What do you think happened? After Jesus grabbed his hand and rescued him from drowning do you think he made him swim back to the boat? I am thinking they had themselves a time out on the waves. Who knows maybe they all got out of the boat then? Hmmm. JESUS is Lord of the sea and everything in it. He is Lord.

DAY 5   READ   Isaiah 55:1-13

1.   What does the Lord offer all who are thirsty and hungry?

2.   What does God's word accomplish?

3.   What is your favorite verse and why?

DAY 6   Fill in ….

	Who believed?	What did they believe?
Hebrews 11:8-10		
Exodus 4:29-31		
Luke 1:45		
John 2:22		

NOTES

FAITH WEEK 12   Father Abraham

I love you, LORD, my strength, LORD, my rock, my fortress, my deliverer, My God, my rock of refuge, my shield, my saving horn, my stronghold! Praised be the LORD, I exclaim! I have been delivered from my enemies. He reached down from on high and seized me; drew me out of the deep waters....He rescued me from my mighty enemy, from foes too powerful for me. They attacked me on a day of distress, but the LORD came to my support. He set me free in the open; He rescued me because He loves me.   ***Psalm 18***

DAY 1

READ   Genesis 11:26-32 and 12:1-5   Abraham's Call & Migration

1.   What did God tell Abram (not yet Abraham) to do?

2.   What did God promise Abram?

3.   What did Abram do? Comment on his faith. See Hebrews 11:8-10

DAY 2

READ   Genesis 17: 1-11

1.   What is the Covenant that God made with Abraham? His name is now changed, how does his name change reflect this Covenant?

2.   What was the sign of the Covenant?

READ   Genesis 15:1-6

3.   What does God promise Abraham?

4.   Describe Abraham's faith. (See Romans 4:18-22)

4.   What did God do for Abraham because of his faith, and us because of our faith ? (See Romans 4:3, Romans 4:22-25, Galatians 3:6-7)

DAY 3

READ Genesis 21:1-14a

1.   What did God command Abraham to do regarding Ishmael?

2.   Describe how Abraham's faith was tested.

DAY 4

READ   Genesis 22:1-19   Abraham and Isaac

1.   When God called Abraham, Abraham replied "READY" What is the significance of this and his leaving first thing in the morning? (See Genesis 22:3)

2.   How is this story a foreshadowing of Jesus and the cross?

3.   Describe Abraham's faith. Describe what he did, what he must have felt, thought. (See Hebrews 11:17-19)

READ   Matthew 17:19-21

4.   Abraham's faith is considered great. How much faith do we need and what can we do with it?

Abraham was called by God to sacrifice his one and only son. The son the Lord promised him. Do you think Abraham believed God could raise him from the dead? If he believed everything God said to him, he would also have to have believed that he would be the father of many, the father of nations. God told Abraham that his descendants would outnumber the stars in the sky or the grains of sand in the sea.

How could Abraham believe that God would ask him to sacrifice his only son and still accomplish this? Sacrifices were a gift to the Lord. God was asking Abraham to give Him his son. It's possible Abraham did not see it as killing. Sacrifices were sacred. Certainly, he must have been absolutely sure that God said it. There could have been no doubt. He didn't seem to waiver, either. He heard from God and obeyed without question. How many times do we waiver? Did God really ask me to give this up?

Father, may we know your will for us just as Abraham knew your will. May we not rest or quit praying until we have that same peace and certainty that Abraham had. Help us to press into you and your will for us.

DAY 5

READ Acts 3:1–16 Cure of the Crippled Beggar

1. Whose faith cured the crippled man?

2. Where did Peter's faith come from? (see Mark 16:20, Acts 2:4, Acts 3:1, Acts 1:14)

3. How can we have the same faith Peter had?

4. Who does Peter give the GLORY to? Does Peter believe he healed the man; does he want recognition? Who gets the credit?

DAY 6

READ Notes on following page

1. Comment about something you learned or found enlightening.

Reflection

THE LAME MAN - When Peter and John went to pray, they met a lame man on the way. What incredible things happen when you are on your way to prayer? Especially when you make a habit of it as these apostles did? They were on their way to the Temple, the Bible says, for the Three O'clock hour of prayer. Wouldn't it be nice if we scheduled an hour of prayer in our homes or church each day? Imagine the miracles; imagine who might show up, what might happen?

Peter and John met a lame man on the way. The man was put there by someone, probably a family member, maybe someone who is profiting from him, we don't know, but every day he lay down at the gate in order to beg. He was looking for help. He couldn't help himself; he could only rely on the generosity and pity of others. He was at their mercy.

When he saw Peter and John and how they looked at him, he was sure he was going to receive something. The Bible said they looked intently at the beggar. I am sure most who passed him kept their eyes on the road or feigned preoccupation. They didn't want to have to say no, or maybe by now they were so used to him they didn't even notice him. I can imagine his hope when Peter and John paid attention to him. Peter said something like this to the beggar; "I have no money, no silver, no gold, but what I do have I give you..."

Maybe it was a good thing Peter and John were without money. If they had money, maybe they would have given it, and the beggar would remain a beggar and lame. The man needed Jesus, and thankfully, that is what they offered him. Peter took the man by the right hand and raised him up. What faith in God Peter had! He knew God was with him, in him. Peter was one with God. He knew without a doubt that God wanted to heal this man. He wouldn't have been so bold if he didn't know God would come through when he said those words. He said, "In the name of Jesus Christ of Nazareth, rise up and walk." Then he took his hand and pulled him up.

WOW, what faith! I just wonder what was going on between God and Peter and John at the time. I would love to have heard the conversation. Were they ready, are they always ready when God wants to move? Or were they praying for this man for weeks or maybe months? I am sure they saw him every day. Were they waiting on God? Did they hear something special from God that day? Were they filled with the Holy Spirit? Were they always available to be used by God? Did they work hand in hand with God? Is God waiting for us to be ready, available? Are we truly His hands and feet?

NOTES

FAITH WEEK 13   Lack of Faith

Do not be anxious about anything, but in everything, by prayer and petition, with thanksgiving, present your requests to God. And the peace of God, which transcends all understanding, will guard your hearts and your minds in Christ Jesus.   Philippians 4:6-7

—❖—❖—❖—

Lord Jesus, I am trusting in you and anxious for nothing. I am praying and presenting to you my requests believing that you hear me and thanking you ahead of time. May your peace Father which transcends all understanding guard my heart and mind in Christ Jesus my Lord.

Day 1
READ   Joshua 1:1-18
1.   What does God ask Joshua to do?

2.   What does God promise Joshua? (See verses 1-9)

READ   Joshua 1:10-11 and 16-18
3.   What does God command the Israelites to do?

4.   What land is the Lord giving you? How does He want you to take possession of it? Ponder this. Ask the Holy Spirit for guidance and the answer.

5.   How do they respond?

This is not the first time God is giving the Israelites the Promised Land. The first time they refused it. They had no faith to receive what the Lord was giving them. When Moses brought the Israelites out of Egypt He promised them He was taking them to a land flowing with milk and honey.

"...so I have decided to lead you up out of the misery of Egypt into the land of the Canaanites, Hittites, Amorites, Perizzites, Hivites and Jebusites, a land flowing with milk and honey." **Ex 3:17**

DAY 2

READ   Numbers 13:1-33

1.   Summarize the accounts of the scouting trip to the Promised Land.

2.   What did Caleb suggest?

3.   Describe how the Israelites saw themselves compared to the inhabitants of the land. Can you relate?

4.   ** BONUS** What was Moses' wife's name?

DAY 3

READ   Numbers 14:1-9   Revolt in the Wilderness

1.   How did the Israelites as a whole respond to the news from the scouts?

2.   What is the response of Caleb and Joshua?

READ   Numbers 14:10-19
3.   How does God initially react to the peoples' complaints?

4.   Why is God so disappointed?   (See Deuteronomy 7:17-19)

5.   What did God offer Moses?

6.   What do you think of Moses?

DAY 4
READ   Numbers 14:20-38
1.   How does God judge the Israelites?

2.   Why is God so harsh? (See Numbers 14:22 and Numbers 14:11-12)

3.   How does God favor Joshua and Caleb and why?

4.   Why are the words of our mouth so important? (verse 28). See also Proverbs 21:23

Pray these scripture verses.

Psalm 141:3 *Set a guard over my mouth, LORD; keep watch over the door of my lips.*

Psalm 19:14 *May these words of my mouth and this meditation of my heart be pleasing in your sight, LORD, my Rock and my Redeemer.*

Proverbs 21:23 *Those who guard their mouths and their tongues keep themselves from calamity.*

DAY 5
READ   Numbers 16

1.   What was Korah's, Dathan's, and Abiram's complaint?

2.   Who did they revolt against?

3.   How were Moses and God united in doling out the punishment?

4.   What happened to Korah, Dathan and Abiram and their respective families?

Jealousy and Numbers 16

We have all felt jealousy at one time or other and know how dangerous and destructive it can be. Perhaps a sister or brother gets all the "new stuff" growing up, a sibling gets more attention from a parent, a friend or co-worker purchases a new car, dress, home……, a friend's husband is so much more understanding and kinder than yours, a neighbor's child gets accepted into a great college and with a scholarship. These are just a few examples of ways that jealousy slips into our lives. I use the word "slip" because it enters so quietly, stealthily, without a sound. It starts with a thought, an idea, a feeling, and if we let it, before we know it we are consumed. Like the characters in this bible story, jealousy can destroy you.

Korah, Dathan, and Abiram were so concerned with what they didn't have; they couldn't see what God had given them. Moses was appointed by God. And God gave him the leadership and the position. K, D, and A couldn't see that they also had gifts from God, and instead, they let their jealousy of Moses blind them. They couldn't, or refused to, understand that God had given Moses certain blessings and graces, and they had also received talents and blessings from God as well.

God gives us all gifts and talents. It is a challenge to understand and find your true talents in this life. Seek and find who you are and use it for the glory of God. Focus on that, not on what others have that might appear to be larger or grander. And you'll be amazed at what God shows you and where He takes you!

Written by: Kate Johnston

DAY 6

READ John 11:41-53

1. Describe the unbelief.

2. What did Caiaphas prophecy? Comment.

READ John 10:22-28

3. Who believes and who doesn't? Comment.

4.   Comment on reflection below.

Reflection

NO COMPLAINING ALLOWED.

This sign is on Pope Francis' door. It was a gift from a
psychologist. It translates: "It is forbidden to complain,"
according to the "Catholic News Agency."

Complaining gets you nowhere and keeps you where you are.
Complaining is the same as doubting. When you complain, you
are describing your situation as dire, as if you have no hope, and
have not reached out to God. Complaining is against God
because you are acting like you don't trust God to come through for you. Complaining is faithless.
Complaining is hopeless.

Joyce Meyer coined this phrase, "Complain and remain or praise and be raised." When we complain,
we remain in whatever situation we are complaining about. You can't rise above your confession.
Whatever comes out of your mouth is an expression of what is in your heart. Whatever you are full of
comes out of you eventually. When complaining comes out of you, it's because you are full of
negativity and doubt and fear.

> **Matthew 12:34-37**
> *For from the fullness of the heart the mouth speaks. [35] A good person brings forth good
> out of a store of goodness, but an evil person brings forth evil out of a store of evil. [36] [y]I
> tell you, on the day of judgment people will render an account for every careless word
> they speak. [37] By your words you will be acquitted, and by your words you will be
> condemned."*

I used to wake up and sit up in bed every morning, and a complaint would escape me. "UGGGH" or
"I hate getting up," or "I hate Mondays." What a horrible way to begin the day. Every time we let a
complaint out, it curses our day. The more you complain, the longer you remain. If you complain
about how bad Mondays are, they will remain that way.

Mondays are no different than any other day. We have just decided they are dreadful — our decision
affects our confession (what we are saying), and our confession (what we are saying) affects our
attitude. We hear what comes out of our mouth, and we believe what we hear. Our words reinforce
our feelings and attitudes and beliefs. The Bible tells us that faith comes from hearing. What you are
speaking out of your mouth, you are hearing and believing. What are you hearing? What you are
listening to is what you are going to believe and act on.

When Israel was delivered from slavery and brought to the land God promised them, they refused to enter. They were afraid and complained and grumbled against Moses and God.

God was furious.

Numbers 14:2-4, 10-11, 26-30

Their voices rose in a great chorus of protest against Moses and Aaron. "If only we had died in Egypt, or even here in the wilderness!" they complained. 3 "Why is the Lord taking us to this country only to have us die in battle? Our wives and our little ones will be carried off as plunder! Wouldn't it be better for us to return to Egypt?" 4 Then they plotted among themselves, "Let's choose a new leader and go back to Egypt!".....

Then the glorious presence of the Lord appeared to all the Israelites at the Tabernacle. [11 And the Lord said to Moses, "How long will these people treat me with contempt? Will they never believe me, even after all the miraculous signs I have done among them? .... 26 Then the Lord said to Moses and Aaron, 27 "How long must I put up with this wicked community and its complaints about me? Yes, I have heard the complaints the Israelites are making against me.

28 Now tell them this: 'As surely as I live, declares the Lord, I will do to you the very things I heard you say. 29 You will all drop dead in this wilderness! Because you complained against me, every one of you who is twenty years old or older and was included in the registration will die. 30 You will not enter and occupy the land I swore to give you. The only exceptions will be Caleb son of Jephunneh and Joshua son of Nun.

Why was God so furious? He was angry with them because of their lack of faith in Him and in His promise to bring them into the land He had promised them. This was the same group of people who just experienced the ten plagues in Egypt. This is the same group of people who saw God turn the Nile River to blood and part the Red Sea. How could they so soon afterward doubt Him?

Be careful not to complain. It could be hazardous to your health. Whatever you complain about may just happen. God gave Israel just what they said. They said they were going to die in the desert, so God let it happen. He told them that they would have exactly what they are complaining they will have.

Don't say ,"I hate my house" you may lose it. Don't say, "I hate my life" it opens the door to the devil. Be grateful instead. If you complain, as we all do, catch yourself and be determined to quit. God cannot advance a complainer. God cannot take you to a new level of faith and leadership if you can't embrace where He has you now.

When complaining grips you and tempts you, do the opposite. The moment you feel a complaint coming out of your mouth, stop and begin to praise God instead. Thank God for something. Praise God for who He is and what He has done for you. Tell Him how much you love him. Complaining comes naturally, but Praise does not, so it needs to be intentional.

Now when I get out of bed, I begin each day praising God. I will not let "UGGGH" come out of my mouth. The very moment it does, I change my words and ask God to forgive me. I don't want God to think I am ungrateful for all I have. How dare I complain when God has given me everything? *"Until now you have not asked anything in my name; ask and you will receive, so that your joy may be complete."* **John 16: 24**

God has great plans for your future. He promises you and me a future full of hope. Are you sick or fearful and tempted to complain? Listen instead to the word of God. It will supernaturally feed you and lift you up.

NOTES

FAITH WEEK 14   Faith-filled History

Then David blessed the LORD in the presence of the whole assembly,
praying in these words: "Blessed may you be, O LORD, God of Israel our father, from eternity to
eternity." Yours, O LORD, are grandeur and power, majesty, splendor, and glory. For all in heaven
and on earth is yours; yours, O LORD, is the sovereignty; you are exalted as head over all. "Riches
and honor are from you, and you have dominion over all. In your hand are power and might; it is
yours to give grandeur and strength to all. Therefore, our God, we give you thanks and we praise the
majesty of your name." David praised the LORD in the presence of the whole assembly, saying,
"Praise be to you, O LORD, God of our father Israel, **1 Chron 29:10-13**

DAY 1

READ   Daniel 3:1-24 This is a story about the faith of three Israelites

1.   How and why did Shadrach, Meshach and Abednego stand up to King Nebuchadnezzar?

2.   Why is the king so furious with them?

READ   Daniel 3: 46-51 and 3:90-97 NAB

3.   Describe what happened to them in the fire.

4.   Describe King Nebuchadnezzar's response to their deliverance from the fire.

5.   What did you learn about faith in these scriptures?

DAY 2

 Joshua was instructed by God to take over after Moses died. God assures Joshua that He will be with Joshua just like He was with Moses. Joshua will lead the Israelites into the promised land. Read the following passage from Joshua Chapter 1.

A Reading from Joshua Chapter 1

After Moses, the servant of the LORD, had died, the LORD said Moses' aide Joshua, son of Nun: "My servant Moses is dead. So prepare to cross the Jordan here, with all the people into the land I will give the Israelites. As I promised Moses, I will deliver to you every place where you set foot. Your domain is to be all the land of the Hittites, from the desert and from Lebanon east to the great river Euphrates and west to the Great Sea. No one can withstand you while you live. I will be with you as I was with Moses: I will not leave you nor forsake you, be firm and steadfast, so that you may give this people possession of the land which I swore to their fathers I would give them. Above all, be firm and steadfast, taking care to observe the entire law which my servant Moses enjoined on you. Do not swerve from it either to the right or to the left, that you may succeed wherever you go. Keep this book of the law on your lips. Recite it by day and by night, that you may observe carefully all that is written in it; then you will successfully attain your goal. I command you: be firm and steadfast! Do not fear nor be dismayed, for the LORD, your God, is with you wherever you go."   JOSHUA   Chapter 1

READ   Joshua 3: 5-17

1.   How did God show He was with Joshua and why? Comment. (See also Joshua 1:5 and 5:1)

READ   Joshua 5:2-12 The Israelites celebrate their last Passover in the wilderness!

2.   What happened before they entered the promised land?

3.   What happened to the manna and why?

DAY 3

READ   Joshua Chapter 6

1.   What do you think the Israelites were thinking on the 5th and 6th day of marching?

2.   What do you think the people of Jericho were thinking? (See Joshua 2:9-11)

3.   How did they march? What did they do and what was the significance of the horns?

4.   What happened on the 7th day? Was God true to His Word?

This is a true story.

The fantastic story of the fall of Jericho really happened. The arrival into the Promised Land took place 40 years after the Israelites were confined to the wilderness. At Jericho, the Israelites take the land God promised them as the walls of Jericho fell before them. The city of Jericho was defenseless when the walls surrounding the city crumbled at the hand of God.

When reading the Old Testament, we learn of the punishment of whole nations destroyed by the Israelites. The people of God fought and killed real people but it helps to know they were wicked and receiving just punishment. They were condemned by their decisions and actions long before the nation of Israel/Judah defeated them.

It is helpful to know, as you read the Old Testament, that Israel's enemies were physical while in the New Testament, our enemies are spiritual, described in the Bible as "principalities, powers, world rulers of this present darkness, and evil spirits in the heavens." The Bible says we wrestle not with flesh and blood but with Satan and his demonic powers. In the Old Testament, these rulers, powers and authorities were physical enemies.

We no longer face this kind of punishment and condemnation because we are "IN CHRIST." It is hard for us to see the people sentenced in the Old Testament, but we have to trust God. The more you read the Old Testament, the more the "HOLY SPIRIT" will reveal to you the mysteries of His ways. He is not trying to keep them from you; it just may not be the right time. If God were to reveal to us His word all at once, we would become overwhelmed because it is too great a revelation for us to handle. He reveals to us what we can handle at the present time, so be patient and remain reading His word even when you don't understand. You will as you persevere.

When I don't understand God's word, I ask for revelation from the Holy Spirit. If He gives it to me, great, but many times I am just not ready, or He will give me just a glimpse, just enough to keep me excited. If God was small enough to be understood, He would not be big enough to worship. Moses wanted to see God. God said to Moses something like this, "okay I will reveal myself to you for a moment, but first, I have to wrap you up in a rock, and then I will pass by."

God told Moses that he would only be able to see His back, and then only a glimpse. Moses walked with God; the Bible says closer than any other human being! Yet this was all he could take of GOD. See Exodus 33:18-23 for the story. God is huge, so be satisfied with that when you don't understand, and you will grow. Keep pursuing, and He will keep revealing. God has a breakthrough coming your way. The Israelites waited 40 years, but they were not disappointed. God is not in the disappointing business. The longer you wait the bigger he surprise. You too will have walls coming down. Just wait. Wait hopeful, expectant and in faith.

OPTIONAL - For further study on why God destroys Israel's enemies.

READ   Deuteronomy 7:1-16

5.   What is one reason why God destroyed Israel's enemies? (see Dt. 7:16,10)

READ   Deuteronomy 9:1-6 Deuteronomy 20:16-18

6.   What is another reason God destroyed Israel's enemies? (See Dt 9:4-5)

DAY 4

READ   Judges 6:11-16 Gideon

1.   What did God call Gideon? Did Gideon fit the description?

2.   Why did God choose Gideon?

READ   Judges 6:33-40, 7:1-7

3.   Why did God reduce the army?

4.   Do we give God the glory He deserves?

DAY 5

READ   1 Kings 16:29-33 and 1 Kings 17:1-7

1.   Describe how Ahab angered the Lord. (See 1Kings 21:23-26)

2.   Why did God stop the rain? (See Leviticus 26:1-6)

3.   What was the condition of the land? (See 1 Kings:17:7)

READ 1 Kings 18:1-8, 1 Kings 18:16-18

4. Ahab blames Elijah for the drought. How does Elijah counter that charge?

READ 1 Kings 18:19-29

5. Why is Elijah putting their gods to the test?

6. Why is Elijah mocking the prophets of Baal?

DAY 6

READ 1 Kings 18: 30-39

1. What does Elijah pray?

2. What did the people do when they realized that the God of Abraham, Isaac, and Jacob is the true GOD?

3. Comment on this scripture as the Lord reveals Himself to you.

4.   Comment on notes on the following page.

Reflection

In the Bible we hear how God comforts Joshua when he is afraid. Joshua was in charge of the Israelites after Moses had died, and he is afraid of leading the people. He hears God calling Him and yet he feels fear. In the first chapter of Joshua, God wants Joshua to lead the people across the river Jordan and He promises He will be with Joshua always as He was with Moses. God says to Joshua: "I command you, be firm and steadfast! Do not fear nor be dismayed, for the Lord, your God, is with you wherever you go."

Instead of being afraid, God wants Joshua to be unshakeable, unswerving in devotion, loyal in the face of trouble and difficulty. The Lord is my light and my salvation, whom do I fear? Though an army encamps against me, my heart shall not fear; though war rise up against me yet I will be confident. **Psalm 27:1,3** If you keep this and similar scriptures in the forefront of your mind, you fill your mind with faith and eliminate the space where fear once resided. In **Isaiah 41:10** God promises, "For I am the Lord, your God, who takes hold of your right hand and says to you, do not fear. I will help you."

Isn't this awesome? The most powerful, the smartest, the most loving WANTS to help us. In return, God wants us to trust Him completely. Fear and trust are opposites. When you are frozen in fear, you cannot abide in trust. When you feel afraid, turn to Scripture. We hear in **Psalm 34:5** I sought the LORD, and he answered me, and delivered me from all my fears. When you turn to God, you are stepping out in faith and you must believe he will deliver you. He promises to. When you give your fear over to God, He gives you the gift of faith in exchange. (Excerpts from teaching on Fear)

Written by Julie Blaskovich

NOTES

FAITH WEEK 15   Faith in Jesus

And when you pray, do not keep on babbling like pagans, for they think they will be heard because of their many words. Do not be like them, for your Father knows what you need before you ask him. "This, then, is how you should pray:"

"Our Father in heaven, hallowed be your name, your kingdom come, your will be done on earth as it is in heaven. Give us today our daily bread. Forgive us our debts, as we also have forgiven our debtors. And lead us not into temptation, but deliver us from the evil one.' *Matthew 6:7-13*

DAY 1

READ   1 John 5:1-12

    1.   Who is begotten by God?

    2.   What is the love of God? (See Gospel of John 15:verses 12 and 17)

    3.   What does our faith accomplish?

    4.   Who conquers the world and how?

RE - READ   1 John 5:7-12

5.   What was God's testimony concerning Jesus?

READ   Matthew 17:13 (See also Gospel of John 1:32-34)

6.   Can we doubt that God sent Jesus? Comment.

DAY 2

READ   James 1:1-8

1.   What does the scripture teach you about faith?

READ   James 2:14-26

2.   What is the relationship between faith and works? Describe one.

DAY 3

READ   Proverbs 3:1-6

1.   What does God promise us when we trust in Him? (See Psalm 125:1-2, Psalm 32:6-10, Psalm 37:3-6 and Isaiah 26:3-4)

DAY 4

READ   each of the following scriptures

1.   What things are we tempted to put our trust in?

Jeremiah 48:7   _____

Psalm 20:7-9   _____

Psalm 118:8-9   _____

Ezek 16:4-16   _____

Jeremiah 17:5   _____

Comment:

Resting in him…. Jesus says to rest in Him.

I found my mother (age 81) the other day in the den "resting" in her rocker after a long day of busyness: errands, cooking, gardening, cleaning, etc…. She was so tired, and I thought she was just sitting and reading. However she was doing so much more than that. She was resting and reading a devotional; she was "resting in Him." That's what Jesus means when He tells us to rest in Him. Leave our busyness, our errands, our cares, and take time out from our lives to do nothing for a bit and rest in Him: in His comfort, calm, peace, security, and love. When we do that, we are putting our trust in Him and saying, "Lord, I'm putting it all aside and resting and trusting in you to do what's best." Only in resting in Him will we find true, everlasting peace.

"Come to me, all you who labor and are burdened, and I will give you rest." **Matthew 11:28**

Written by: Kate Johnston

DAY 5
READ   Romans 10:8-17

1.   Have you ever confessed out loud, to others, that Jesus is your Lord?

2.   How can we find the courage to do it?

3.   What do these scriptures say we need to do to be saved?

4.   Where does faith come from? See also Acts 14:8-10.

DAY 6
READ   John 14: 8-14

1.   How do we know the Father?

2.   What can we do through Jesus?

Do you hear what Jesus is saying to us? **John chapter 14:12-14** says, *"Amen, Amen, I say to you, whoever believes in me will do the works that I do, and will do even greater ones than these, because I am going to the Father. And whatever you ask in my name, I will do, so that the Father may be glorified in the Son. If you ask anything of me in my name, I will do it."*

He doesn't say "almost anything" or "anything but"... we always say but... He doesn't say but. Do you know how our Father in heaven receives glory? He receives glory from His Son, who wants to bring Him glory here on earth. He wants the world to know His Father. Jesus wants the world to know and trust and believe in His Father. He wants everyone to know His goodness and love for them so that they, too, may experience His love and peace.

He says it again in **John 15:7-8** *"If you remain in me and my words remain in you, ask for whatever you want, and it will be done for you. By this is my Father glorified, that you bear much fruit and become my disciples."*

HOW does Jesus bring Glory to His Father? Through us. What a privilege to be part of it. EVERY TIME WE ASK, God has the opportunity to shine in the world. God has made it, so we are involved in His work here on earth. He includes us in what He does. We are Jesus' hands and feet to a dry and thirsty world. Go into all the world and proclaim the good news with faith!!!

Comments:

NOTES

Spirit Filled Catholic Bible Study Series

Contact us at www.spiritfilledcatholic.com

Marybeth Wuenschel
972-832-7260
mbwuenschel@gmail.com

Follow us on Facebook
Catholic Bible Study

https://www.facebook.com/catholicdevotional/

BIBLIOGRAPHY

New American Bible source – United States Conference of Catholic Bishops

http://www.usccb.org/nab/bible/index.shtml

All other Bible translations   -   Biblegateway

http://www.biblegateway.com

Spirit Filled Catholic